HOW TO IMPROVE
GOVERNANCE

HOW TO IMPROVE
GOVERNANCE

A New Framework
for Analysis and Action

DAVID DE FERRANTI, JUSTIN JACINTO,
ANTHONY J. ODY, AND GRAEME RAMSHAW

BROOKINGS INSTITUTION PRESS
Washington, D.C.

Library of Congress Cataloging-in-Publication data

How to improve governance : a new framework for analysis and action / David de Ferranti ...[et al.].
     p.   cm.
   Includes bibliographical references and index.
   Summary: "Emphasizes the need for a comprehensive analytical framework that considers transparency, accountability, governance, and corruption throughout the calculus. Discusses how it can be applied to different countries to help analyze the current situation and identify potential areas for improvement, assessing their relative feasibility and the steps needed to promote them"—Provided by publisher.
   ISBN 978-0-8157-0283-2 (pbk. : alk. paper)
   1. Government accountability. 2. Transparency in government. 3. Political corruption—Prevention. 4. Government accountability—Case studies. 5. Transparency in government—Case studies. 6. Political corruption—Prevention—Case studies.. I. De Ferranti, David M. II. Title.

   JF1351.H685 2009
   352.8'8—dc22   2009008080

9 8 7 6 5 4 3 2 1

The paper used in this publication meets minimum requirements of the American National Standard for Information Sciences—Permanence of Paper for Printed Library Materials: ANSI Z39.48-1992.

Typeset in Minion

Composition by Cynthia Stock
Silver Spring, Maryland

Printed by Versa Press
East Peoria, Illinois

Contents

APPENDIXES: COUNTRY CASE STUDIES

Acknowledgments

This study, undertaken as part of the Transparency and Accountability Project with funding from the Hewlett Foundation, benefited from ideas and inputs from the many groups and individuals who were consulted, including those who participated in roundtable sessions and other meetings in Washington, D.C., and elsewhere. Numerous reviewers of the work, many of whom were also among those consulted, contributed invaluable comments and suggestions that are reflected in the final product here. Many colleagues at the Brookings Institution and the Results for Development Institute provided invaluable support and guidance.

The authors are extremely grateful to all these individuals and their organizations for giving generously of their time and talent. While it is impossible to mention them all by name, several are deserving of special mention: Smita Singh, Linda Frey, and C. R. Hibbs for providing the initial impetus for this research and for their consistent support throughout its progress; Paul Collier, Tom Heller, Susan Rose Ackerman, Frank Fukuyama, Bjoern Dressel, Warren Krafchik, and Vinod Vyasulu for their insightful criticisms and suggestions; and Charles Griffin and Joan Santini for their tireless work in making this project and this study a success.

PART

I

The Challenge

1 | *Introduction*

An African cabinet minister was recently visited by separate teams of eager-to-help foreigners over a three-month period. One team extolled the importance of strengthening transparency in public affairs. A second had similar counsel on accountability, a third on good governance, and a fourth on fighting corruption.[1] Each had a ready-to-roll package of recommended actions.

Some advocated supply-side measures, so-called because they seek to improve the performance of governments, the suppliers of governance. Create or improve specially empowered government bodies, some said. Or redraw the government structurally, get more training for bureaucrats, adopt better laws (for example, freedom of information laws), fix the courts system, bolster enforcement, and bring in external expertise.

Others espoused demand-side initiatives that focus on the impact that entities outside government can have, working in support of citizens' desire— indeed, *demand*—for better public institutions. Strengthen independent groups (nongovernmental organizations [NGOs] and think tanks) to serve as watchdogs of the public budgets, some urged. Improve the capacity of the media—print, broadcast, and online—to expose governmental deficiencies. Clean up electoral processes. Empower citizens more, ensuring that marginalized populations have a real vote and the opportunity to express their voice.

The Problem

The minister, a reformer, welcomed the offers of help, correctly reading in them the international development community's recent explosion of attention to these matters. But the minister was troubled for several reasons.

3

First, there was no common analytical framework for understanding the interrelations among transparency, accountability, governance, and anticorruption (and other ideas that could be added to this list, such as promotion of democracy). It was not easy to define exactly what each of the four concepts really meant or to pin down the differences and similarities among them. The four teams were unaware of each other's visits, and each was unable to explain how the various sets of ideas fit together. The pieces of the puzzle were plain to see, but no one knew how to put them together.

Second, it seemed as if solutions were being touted without a careful diagnosis of the situation in this particular country to assess the real problems and most urgent priorities. The proponents of "work on improving government itself" wanted to get on with restructuring and retraining—to fix a problem whose complexities had not been delineated. The "strengthen independent watchdogs" activists were keen to start building up their target groups. The anticorruption missionaries, the transparency buffs, and others had their respective agendas fixed as well.

Third, and related to this, there was no appreciation of the fact that, if careful diagnosis were performed, different prescriptions might emerge for different situations. In some country circumstances, supply-side measures might make eminent sense, but in others they might get nowhere. Likewise, in some countries, strengthening watchdog groups might be a key priority, while elsewhere it might prove a waste of time until other constraints had been eased. Unrecognized was the crucial notion that promoting good governmental performance requires many interconnected components, like the links of a chain. So was the further point that, as with any chain, it may make sense to look to see where the weakest links are and work on fixing those first.

Fourth, even if all these considerations were fully understood, there was no readily usable diagnostic tool—no practical methodology—for carrying out an adequate assessment of a particular country context so that the most appropriate actions could be chosen. There was no accepted process for identifying the weak links, no guidance on who had to do what and how long it might take to come up with results.

The minister's story epitomizes what many countries are now facing and pinpoints the purpose of this volume. In the wake of the burst of effort on transparency, accountability, governance, and anticorruption in the last five years, a variety of important initiatives is now being put into action across the world.[2] With this outpouring has come a need for clear advice on how to tackle these issues all together and on how they fit, conceptually and practically, within the larger set of development objectives and problems that countries grapple with.

In the meanwhile, efforts to combat corruption, in which case-based investigative and enforcement concerns are necessarily prominent, have evolved very differently from work on transparency, in which setting standards and naming-and-shaming activities have needed to be stressed. Research and debate on accountability, governance, and related concepts such as corporate responsibility and public sector reform have taken other turns. The result has been separate conversations, in isolation from each other, with too little exploration of commonalities and wider development linkages.

The story told by the African minister could be multiplied. There are many countries that set out to implement reforms to improve their governance standards, but they fail for one reason or another to meet their goals. Four such examples, each a composite of the experiences of multiple countries, can help illustrate dimensions of the larger challenge:

—The African country whose new leaders introduced a range of reforms, recommended by experts from industrialized countries, including efforts to make more information about government available to the citizens: the experts predicted that progress would follow, but they failed to take into account the society's long-standing cultural taboos on aggressive questioning of those in authority;

—The Latin American country that passed a freedom of information act, while also taking complementary measures to make information available in usable form: however, the experts failed to appreciate that many among the poorer elements in the society, defined largely by ethnicity, continued to face serious barriers to any form of meaningful political participation;

—The Asian country whose reformers, full of good intentions, nonetheless stalemated each other with their competing ideas over priorities and also could not agree on how to neutralize the influence of vested interests strongly opposed to reform: as a result, the country ended up with a disparate array of weak reforms, which failed to achieve change of any great importance;

—The middle-income country whose leadership wrongly convinced itself that corruption must be behind the failure of increased appropriations to improve materially the services at a major hospital: alone among the four cases, this is a partial success story—investigations revealed no corruption but opaque accounting and decisionmaking systems that potentially lent themselves to reform.[3]

These four examples illuminate how conventional thinking is often not up to the task of guiding a country's thinking and actions that are needed to reform the relationship between public institutions and the citizenry. The examples show not only that those reforms must be country specific, but also that effective country-specific reforms depend on careful analysis throughout the process of diagnosis, prescription, and implementation.

This book makes the case for the importance of an overall analytical framework that can be applied to different countries to help analyze the current situation, identify potential areas for improvement, and assess their relative feasibility and the steps needed to promote them. The absence of such an overall analytical framework was a fundamental reason for the failures in the four examples. Without an analytic framework, a reform attempt will founder for lack of a shared understanding of the underlying problems and of the feasible reforms. The lack of a compass to describe the country situation currently—and what it would be if the proposed reforms were or were not taken—can result in disastrous missteps. A country-specific analysis needs to be comprehensive, in the sense that it includes the four concepts of transparency, accountability, governance, and anticorruption throughout the calculus.

Defining Terms

Transparency, accountability, governance, and anticorruption are complex concepts, fuzzily understood by some who use them and all the more so when translated into languages other than English. The definitions used in the proposed framework are illustrated in table 1-1, along with related information on associated strengthening initiatives and the actors and programs involved. To expand on these distinctions:

—*Transparency* represents a means to larger ends. Some degree of transparency is a necessary condition for accountability, since those seeking to hold government accountable must be able to observe what government is actually doing. Transparency is also itself a contributor to good governance and an impediment to corruption: "sunlight is the best disinfectant."

—*Accountability* describes the essence of the relationship between the government and those who are governed; the greater the accountability, the more the government responds to the needs and expectations of the public it serves. Efforts to increase accountability rely on transparency—as well as other inputs such as citizen voice, social capital, and democratic processes. Efforts to increase accountability target corruption as well as noncorruption-related shortcomings in government performance including inefficiency and lack of equity. Successful drives for greater accountability improve governance.

Table 1-1. *Definitions, Initiatives, Actors, and Programs*

Definition	Typical strengthening initiatives	Examples of actors and programs
Transparency describes the availability and increased flow to the public of timely, comprehensive, relevant, high-quality and reliable information concerning government activities.[a]	Disclosure of budgets, audits, policies, executive actions, and so on Adoption of policies concerning freedom of information and access to documents Citizen attendance and participation in meetings	Extractive Industries Transparency Initiative Transparency International Revenue Watch Institute International Budget Partnership
Control of corruption describes efforts to prevent the abuse of public office for private gain, including officials accepting, soliciting, or extorting bribes; engaging in patronage and nepotism; appropriating state assets; or improperly diverting state revenues.	Stakeholder consultations Increased reporting and auditing requirements Adoption and enforcement of anticorruption laws with criminal and civil sanctions Oversight by civil society organizations (CSOs)	UN Convention against Corruption European Union Accession Monitoring Program Multilateral and bilateral aid monitoring controls Transparency International Revenue Watch Institute
Accountability, in general, describes the responsiveness on the part of government to citizens' demands concerning the type of public services the public sector should provide. This may include the government's response to citizen efforts to bring about a change in the	Media coverage, including reporting by investigative journalists Creation of independent courts, inspectors general, ombudsmen, and auditors Increase of parliamentary oversight Reform of the electoral process	Performance-based aid programs that withhold funding from governments that are not responsive to their citizens' needs World Bank public expenditure reviews that evaluate whether government resources are used efficiently for their intended purposes

(continues)

Table 1-1 *(continued)*

Definition	Typical strengthening initiatives	Examples of actors and programs
government's behavior by persuasion, demand, or compulsion.[b]	Development of social movements and independent monitoring organizations and networks	CIVICUS: World Alliance for Citizen Participation
		Electoral reform programs
	Strengthening the independent media	Foundation grant programs that support CSOs seeking to influence government
	Application of pressure from external and international NGOs	
Governance describes the overall manner in which public officials and institutions acquire and exercise their authority to shape public policy and provide public goods and services.	Reform of institutions	Multilateral and bilateral capacity-building programs
	Increased transparency and accountability	
		IMF public financial management frameworks
	Anticorruption controls	
		All programs and actors listed above

a. Further discussion of definitions of *government transparency* can be found in A. Fung, with M. Graham, and D. Weil, *Full Disclosure: The Perils and Promise of Transparency* (Cambridge University Press, 2007); A. Florini, ed., *The Right to Know: Transparency for an Open World* (Columbia University Press, 2007).

b. *Accountability* is a tricky term, and we have included our definition above. Readers looking for further efforts to define it should consult Andreas Schedler, "Conceptualizing Accountability," in *The Self-Restraining State: Power and Accountability in New Democracies,* edited by Andreas Schedler, Larry Diamond, and Marc F. Platter (Boulder, Colo.: Lynne Rienner Publishers, 1999), chapter 2.

—*Control of corruption* efforts is oriented to the ends, focused as they are on one specific aspect of poor governance.

—*Governance* is the broadest of these concepts, representing the overall quality of the relationship between citizens and government, which includes responsiveness, efficiency, honesty, and equity. Efforts to increase transparency and accountability contribute to better governance, and anticorruption efforts seek to correct a specific aspect of bad governance. That said, efforts to increase transparency and accountability and anticorruption initiatives do

Figure 1-1. *The Relationship between Transparency, Accountability, Corruption Control, and Governance*

not necessarily address *all* aspects of governance. They might not, for example, address the organizational soundness of public institutions. Figure 1-1 illustrates the basic relationships among the four concepts.

For some purposes—including the sections immediately below—it is useful to talk about all four concepts together. In the rest of this book, we will usually refer to *good governance* or just *governance* as encompassing all four concepts.

Historical Perspective

The history of how international development actors came to focus more on governance issues sheds light on the need for clarity that this book seeks to provide. The story can be told from many different perspectives. Civil society initiatives, such as the founding of Transparency International in 1993, certainly represent important steps in the larger evolutionary process. Many observers also see the World Bank's 1989 study on the obstacles to economic and human development in sub-Saharan Africa as a key starting point. That report declared that "underlying the litany of Africa's development problems is a crisis of governance."[4] The concept of governance embedded in that report was quite expansive, perhaps because it reflected substantial input from African scholars whose first-hand experience led them to believe that achieving good governance required moving beyond macroeconomic and administrative management procedures and techniques to deeper issues of state-society relations, such as democratic conditions, citizens' rights, social inclusion, and the equitable management of resources.[5]

The Africa report and its assertion that the governance problem is larger than poor policy and institutional management and that it involves inherent issues of the government's accountability to the public have been very influential. The leading development institutions did not embrace this broader concept of governance right away, however, and only recently have they begun adjusting their operating strategies to tackle the deeper governance issues mentioned above. Why the delay? First, when the report was released in 1989, the Bank and the International Monetary Fund were still largely committed to focusing on macroeconomic policy adjustments that emphasized stabilization, privatization, and liberalization, and the proponents of this approach saw more governance work as an inappropriate distraction. Second, the World Bank, in particular, was wary of becoming involved in political matters in contravention of its Articles of Agreement. The Bank's leadership narrowly defined the areas of governance in which the organization could be involved, so that the focus remained on administrative and macroeconomic reforms with only a modest expansion into public participation issues.[6] Third, the two institutions simply were not set up to work on broader governance issues. By and large, official development aid loans and grants go to governments, which typically have little interest in using those resources to do such things as strengthen the role of independent media, parliaments, or independent monitoring organizations that are seeking to shine a light on government activities and hold the government accountable.

With time, the idea that broader governance reform is critical to achieving development goals attracted increasing attention. In 1997 UN Secretary General Kofi Annan famously declared, "Good governance is perhaps the single most important factor in eradicating poverty and promoting development." The 2000 Millennium Summit declaration announced that "democratic and participatory governance based on the will of the people" is the best way to ensure that economic and human development goals are achieved.[7] Civil society organizations have continued to agitate for more attention to the accountability aspect of governance. For example, one of the key messages from the 2006 International Anti-Corruption Conference in Guatemala was that more attention must be given by international development actors to domestic sources of government accountability.[8]

The development community has now largely adopted the idea that improving governance in a broad sense (that is, focusing on government accountability to the public) must be a central component of efforts to improve economic and human development outcomes. For example, in July 2006, the United Kingdom Department for International Development released a five-year strategy and implementation plan for tackling poverty, which declares that "we will put governance at the centre of our work—focusing on building states that are capable, responsive and accountable to their citizens."[9] In March 2007, the World Bank approved a new high-profile strategy for promoting good governance and fighting corruption that emphasizes the importance of strengthening the role of entities outside of government that can hold governments accountable and provide a "domestic demand" for good governance.[10] Other leading development institutions, such as the U.S. Agency for International Development and the Inter-American Development Bank have similarly embraced this view at a high level.[11]

While these institutions are now on board conceptually, significant uncertainties remain about whether and how they actually will work toward the goal of improved governance in the broad sense. To an extent, as noted above, the three conditions constraining the major development institutions are still present. Further, there are no easy answers as to how to achieve the goals of the new strategies. Recognizing that the pursuit of good governance is shifting them onto new terrain, some in the development community have begun reaching out for lessons and effective strategies to the democracy-building community, which has long been driven by the U.S. Department of State and organizations such as the National Democratic Institute, the International Republican Institute, and IFES (formerly, the International Foundation for Election Systems). The international development community's linkage with those institutions, which are looking more closely at the importance of working toward better development outcomes rather than simply building democracies for the sake of democracy, could bear important fruit, but the democracy builders have been clear in acknowledging that there are no easy answers or cookie-cutter approaches to solving problems of governance. Rather, experience in this area shows that any efforts to improve governance must grapple with divergent country conditions, unique social and political cultures, often deeply entrenched elite interests, and sensitive matters of social equity, all of which make achieving rapid improvements daunting.

Success is also challenged by the relatively dispersed, compartmentalized, and unorganized character of much of the work being done in this area. Transparency, accountability, governance, and corruption control are complex and multifaceted concepts; progress will require action on multiple fronts. Many of the actors involved in this area will understandably focus their efforts on a narrow aspect of good governance for which they have the particular expertise and experience needed to make a difference (for example, training independent journalists or building think tank–type organizations). However, from the perspective of a developing country, the overall set of interventions can appear disorganized and inefficient since different organizations may simultaneously push for reforms in the same areas and sometimes in a mutually incompatible manner.

Despite the challenges, the international development community has planted its flag on the governance issue, and there is growing conviction that improving governance is vital for achieving sustained progress on development. Aid institutions are committed to taking steps to support improvements in governance, and several of them are prepared to allocate significant resources to the cause. While these developments augur well for progress, they also present a substantial risk. Failure to make progress could be a crucial setback if the enthusiasm and resources that are presently being marshaled for the effort are dissipated.

Much is thus at stake. Whether one looks at how to increase domestic demand for good governance, how to make government more accountable to the public, or how to build democratic processes that deliver results, the underlying issues are essentially the same. There is increasing concern worldwide that development outcomes too often have been unsatisfactory and that this is in large part because governments are not effectively working on behalf of their citizens. There is greater consternation as well that, in the absence of meaningful pressures for good governance, politicians and civil servants are freer to pursue personal gain or simply persist in public office without accomplishing results. But as development actors of various types—bilateral and multilateral institutions; as well as NGOs and independent monitoring organizations, such as local monitoring and advocacy groups; private foundations; domestic governments; and other stakeholders—seek to help, more and more of them are calling for a clearer conceptual framework to guide their efforts.

Notes

1. Related to one of the authors, de Ferranti, by an African official, who requested to remain anonymous.

2. Among the many groups doing crucial work in these arenas are Transparency International and its various country chapters; Revenue Watch Institute—and one of its founding partners, Open Society Institute; International Budget Partnership; the anticorruption initiatives of international bilateral and multilateral institutions such as the development banks, the United Kingdom's Department for International Development, and Norway; and exemplary programs in recipient countries.

3. The four country case studies are discussed in greater detail in appendix F.

4. World Bank, *Sub-Saharan Africa: From Crisis to Sustainable Growth: A Long-Term Perspective Study* (Washington, 1989), p. 60.

5. Thandika Mkandawire, "The Itinerary of an Idea," *Development and Cooperation* 31, no. 10 (Oct. 2004).

6. World Bank, *Governance and Development* (Washington, 1992).

7. United Nations General Assembly, "United Nations Millennium Declaration," General Assembly Resolution A/RES/55/2, 55th sess. (September 8, 2000).

8. International Anti-Corruption Conference Council, "Declaration of the 12th International Anti-Corruption Conference" (Guatemala City, November 18, 2006).

9. U.K. Department for International Development, "White Paper: Making Governance Work for the Poor" (London, July 2006), pp. 18–28.

10. World Bank, "Strengthening Bank Group Engagement on Governance and Anticorruption" (Washington, September 8, 2006), p. 47.

11. U.S. Agency for International Development, "At Freedom's Frontiers: A Democracy and Governance Strategic Framework" (Washington, December 2005), p. 8; Inter-American Development Bank, "Strategy for Promoting Citizen Participation in Bank Activities" (Washington, May 19, 2004).

2

Do Transparency, Accountability, Governance, and Corruption Matter?

Before the analytical framework for understanding and strengthening governance is set out, a precursor question needs to be addressed: Does good governance matter? In other words, are there compelling enough reasons to make strengthening governance a priority for the international development community? The answers to these questions have important implications for everything that follows.

For some, transparency, accountability, governance, and anticorruption are desirable ends on their own, regardless of whether they lead to other benefits in terms of how societies function or other positive outcomes. Proponents of this view see support for their position in studies such as *Voices of the Poor,* which, through interviews with tens of thousands of poor people, found that the poor themselves strongly feel that an absence of "power and voice" is a major source of additional suffering in their lives separate from and beyond that imposed by inadequate financial and material resources. As one respondent explained, "It is this feeling of helplessness that is so painful, more painful than poverty itself."[1]

For others, good governance matters primarily because it is a means to other ends. For many of this school, the chief benefit of good governance is the contribution that it makes to improving a society's well-being, broadly defined but definitely including economic and social development. This proposition is especially important from the viewpoint of development institutions, whose primary focus is on improving economic development and reducing poverty.

Of course, the two views are not incompatible. As Amartya Sen argues, empowerment gives poor people a sense of fulfillment that is valuable in its own right, while at the same time increasing their capability to help themselves.[2]

In light of these considerations, this chapter focuses on whether there is evidence that good governance does in fact contribute to improved economic and social well-being. If not, then there may still be other reasons to care about good governance, but a prominent rationale for it will have been rejected, in which case, further analysis would be needed if improving governance is to be considered a priority by people and institutions not already committed to it.

The discussion of whether good governance enhances well-being begins with examination of the evidence on high-level correlations between measures of good governance and core economic and human development measures (for example, per capita gross domestic product or Human Development Index score). It then turns to disaggregated data.

What the Aggregated Evidence Shows

An obvious method of assessing the value of better governance is to look for a correlation between governance measures and development outcome measures across countries. The research in this area has progressed tremendously over the last ten years, and it provides powerful evidence of the importance of good governance to development. However, while the basic theory behind this approach may seem simple, it is complicated by difficult decisions concerning the choice of measures for each side of the correlation.

What Governance Measures Are Appropriate?

A first challenge concerns the measures of the quality of governance that are used in looking for a correlation. The elements of governance are abstract and multifaceted concepts that do not readily lend themselves to measurement. Accordingly, attempts to measure governance performance at a national level must deal with several complicating issues.

Aggregation is an issue because governance issues arise in many different areas and may be measured in many different ways. For example, the level of transparency in a country concerns, among other things, the strength of laws about disclosure and information access, the openness of government deliberations, and the quality of government record-keeping and performance monitoring. If these measures are left disaggregated, then it may be difficult to identify correlations with development outcomes because of the increased noise in the data. However, if they are aggregated then the uncertainty that was already present in the disaggregated measures can be compounded.

Subjectivity is an issue because some attributes of good governance do not present opportunities for measurement through objective measures. While a concept such as economic performance can be measured by reference to relatively standardized criteria like gross domestic product growth or employment generation, a concept such as government accountability may be best evaluated through opinion surveys of the general public or key stakeholders. Such subjective measures are of course widely used and relied on in many contexts. Nevertheless, their use in efforts to identify a correlation between governance and development adds another element of complexity.

Data comparability concerns the fact that the data used to measure the quality of governance can be obtained using different methodologies in different countries. Although the significance of these differences can arguably be diminished through a well-structured aggregation process, they remain a source of additional uncertainty with regard to the validity of efforts to find high-level correlations.

Despite these challenges, significant progress has been made in the compilation of country-level governance measures. The leading set of measures in this area, the World Bank's Worldwide Governance Indicators (WGI; discussed further below), has not been immune to criticism.[3] However, Daniel Kaufmann, Aart Kraay, and the other World Bank staff who maintain the WGI have continuously refined their methodology since initiating the program in 1996, and the WGI are now widely regarded as a highly valuable metric that recognizes the inherent challenges of collecting these types of data.

What Development Outcome Measures Are Appropriate?

Development can mean very different things to different people, and no single measure can accurately capture all of what it means for a country to develop. Is the aim to reduce poverty or to increase economic performance? If it is to reduce poverty, is the focus on improving the lot of the poorest people, wherever they are? The "bottom billion"? Or all those living on less than $2 a day? Or $3 a day? Or is the focus on all the people in the poorest countries? If the target is to increase economic performance, is the focus on raising overall GDP or GDP per capita or perhaps even per capita income for a certain percentage of the poorest people in the country? Should the measure be adjusted for purchasing power parity (PPP)? What about alternative economic performance metrics such as the World Economic Forum's Global Competitiveness Index? Is the focus on long-term economic prospects or short-term performance?

If human well-being is considered the core of development, are any of the available metrics such as the United Nations Development Programme's Human Development Index or Human Poverty Index convincing? Do those measures need to be adjusted in any way? More deeply, is "greater well-being" determined by the individuals themselves who are affected or by outside judges who presume to know what is best for the poor? And what if there is more transparency but less accountability, or some other mix? Or if cost trade-offs have to be made too (for example if x percent of governance improvement costs A and y percent more of something else costs B), which one is better? Ultimately, there is no clearly optimal way to pick one such specification over another to resolve these complexities, and one must make arbitrary choices or pursue multiple outcomes.

Is There Evidence of a Correlation?

Putting measurement complexities to the side for now, the literature on the relationship between governance and development, which has expanded considerably over the last ten years, shows a correlation—indeed, some authors argue, a causal connection—between the quality of governance and development. The leading dataset in this area, the WGI, aggregates metrics produced by the World Bank and other organizations to track six aspects of governance:
—Voice and accountability
—Political stability and absence of violence
—Government effectiveness
—Regulatory quality
—Rule of law
—Control of corruption[4]
While some of these measures of governance speak more to administrative competency than to good governance as defined in this book, several of the measures are good representations of the quality of governance in a country.

Because of the variety of measures that can be used on both the governance and development sides of the formula, numerous combinations arise in the search for a correlation. That variability can introduce some uncertainty; nevertheless, evidence of a correlation is the norm, not the exception. For example, the WGI authors have plotted each of the aspects of governance against per capita GDP (PPP adjusted), and they found strong evidence of a significant correlation, including on a partially disaggregated level for the most clearly governance-related aspects, specifically those concerning control of corruption and voice and accountability.[5] Several other observers have made similar efforts to assess the effects of improved governance against improved development outcomes using variable regressions across a wide range of countries.[6] Although there is noise in the data, in the sense that some countries are outliers overall, or on individual measures, the consensus among observers is that a strong link connects governance to economic development.[7]

Moreover, there is strong evidence that the correlation is not a result of higher income leading to improved governance but rather that improved governance contributes to improved development outcomes.[8] As Daniel Kaufmann explains:

> Our work finds that there is a very strong and causal link from improved governance to higher incomes, which is summarized by the "300 percent development dividend": a country that improves governance by one standard deviation—which is a realistic improvement where political will exists—can expect to more or less triple its annual per capita income in the long run. Conversely, we do not find evidence that there is significant causation in the opposite direction, from per capita income to the quality of governance. Merely acquiring higher incomes (say, due to higher oil prices, for example, or infusion of aid), *per se* will not automatically result in improved governance.[9]

This conclusion is backed by alternative approaches to assessing the value of good governance. For example, efforts to quantify the global cost of corruption range from estimates of $600 billion to $1.5 trillion annually.[10]

What does this mean?

What the Disaggregated Evidence Shows

The evidence that improving governance promotes development and reduces poverty has limitations, however—not the least of which is its highly aggregated nature. Thus additional work continues to be done, including studies that delve into the components of the aggregate relationship. Figure 2-1 illustrates what this entails. The top arrow from "Good governance" to "Greater well-being" (whether defined in terms of economic growth, human development, or poverty reduction) traces the relationship of primary interest here. Although there is support for this relationship from aggregate evidence, additional support—not subject to the same methodological and data challenges—can be derived from breaking down the aggregate into its component parts and examining the evidence on each part individually.

Figure 2-1. *How Good Governance Affects Development Outcomes: Breaking Down the Pathways*

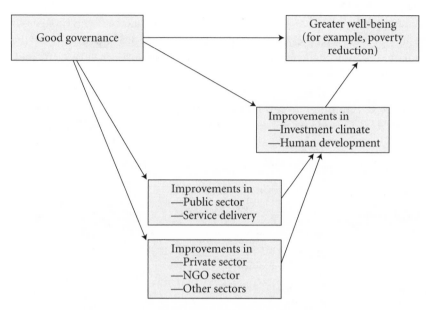

The first breakdown is suggested in the considerable literature on the various factors that contribute to development—literature that includes the succession of annual *World Development Reports* by the World Bank, and other sources.[11] Drawing from that work—and from the different ways that the possibilities are structured there—one plausible view holds that development depends crucially on two broad factors, investment climate and public services, each of which incorporates a host of other factors of a more specific nature. This characterization leads to the second level of arrows in figure 2-1, showing the impact of good governance on the investment climate and on human development, and the impact of those factors, in turn, on well-being. On the latter impact, there is already extensive supportive evidence from numerous development studies.[12] There is also growing support on the former (from good governance to investment climate and human development). However, documenting that impact, though not as difficult as the overall aggregate linkage, is still hard to do in practice.

So a further breakdown helps: tracking the effect that good governance has on the investment climate and human development to the next level of arrows by focusing on governance's impact on public service delivery and the impact of improved public service delivery on the investment climate and human development. (Logically, there must also be linkages through private sector activity, as also shown in figure 2-1.)

As each building block of the effect of good governance is thus broken out and examined separately, additional evidence can be brought to bear, and the methodological challenges become more tractable. A stronger case emerges. Along the way, metrics can be generated that not only shed light on the causal connections but also provide a basis for making comparisons of perform-ance across countries, for example, for "naming and shaming" purposes and for shifting to performance-based aid. Note that, as the arrows between the factors indicate, improvements in one factor can lead to better development outcomes directly or through other intermediate factors.

Linkages through the Investment Climate

A healthy, growing economy, which is essential to sustained progress on devel-opment in general, requires a supportive investment climate.[13] Sometimes known by other names (for example, "enabling environment"), a country's investment climate is the result of the choices it makes in its macro- and microeconomic policies; laws; regulatory structures; judicial system; banking and finance institutions; and all the many other decisions, institutions, and day-to-day practices that determine whether businesses, investors, entrepre-neurs, employers, and markets generally find it easy and attractive, or difficult and unappealing, to take risks and expand. Some of the most critical busi-nesses and investors may be thousands or even millions of small farmers or tiny enterprises. Where the investment climate is favorable, flourishing eco-nomic activity churns out jobs, increased incomes, and growth opportunities that can lift households to higher living standards than they could achieve oth-erwise. Extensive research strongly supports the hypothesis that a favorable investment climate has a powerful positive impact on development.[14]

Further, it makes intuitive sense that transparency and accountability have a strong effect on private investment. Transparency is important to efforts to remove excessive and unnecessary government regulatory requirements that discourage entrepreneurs and investors, since if information about those requirements—and who sets them and how they work to the advantage of some and as barriers to others—is widely available, then investors can better provide constructive input on how the system should be changed to enable more investment.[15] Accountability is critical to private investment, as it is with any government program, in the sense that accountability pressures operate as incentives for government entities (from individual officials to entire regimes) to deliver improvements in private investment lest they be held accountable through electoral processes or other means.[16] Transparency and accountability are perhaps most important to investment climate as a means of curtailing corruption, widely recognized as a major impediment to increased investment.[17]

The data support this positive impact of transparency, accountability, and corruption control. Regarding transparency, one of the key lessons of the World Bank's extensive surveys of private firms in developing countries is that the number one concern of firms doing business in developing countries is uncertainty about the content of government policies and the manner in which they are implemented.[18] Accountability considerations also show up in the data, with firms very concerned about arbitrary implementation of regulations and weak enforcement of contracts and property rights.[19] The links between corruption and investment climate are even more pronounced. One of the first empirical studies, by Paulo Mauro in 1995, provided evidence of a considerable linkage between corruption and investment climate by comparing Business International indexes of corruption with GDP per capita growth rates and investment-GDP ratios.[20] Stephen Keefer and Philip Knack obtained similar results using data from the *International Country Risk Guide.*[21]

The *Doing Business* reports of the World Bank also support the link between good governance and investment. The extensive data in those studies provide cross-country comparisons of the cost and time required to legally perform basic operations of a business—for example, starting an enterprise, terminating one, or enforcing a contract. The differences are stark: in successful advanced economies it takes just a few days to start a business, whereas in developing countries, which are burdened with excessive regulation, it can take many months, which effectively prevents legal entry by new firms that have too little capital to run the gauntlet of roadblocks and come up with the side payments required to get launched.[22]

One of the authors of this book has presented these data extensively to public and private sector leaders in many countries, enabling them to see how their nation stacks up alongside their neighbors and the best-run economies. The initial reaction of the owners of the largest firms in countries with the highest regulatory barriers was that the fault lay entirely with their government, for unnecessarily imposing heavy burdens. But on closer scrutiny, it became clear that government regulators were at least partly responding to—and sometimes restrained by—the large firms' interests in protecting themselves against the entry of upstart competitors. The giants did not want to open the doors to the little guys. But where concerted efforts have been successful in bringing to light the evidence of impediments to enterprise and in rectifying them (that is, where transparency and accountability are strong), the barriers are coming down, and the results are showing up in the most recent *Doing Business* numbers.[23]

A further link between governance quality and the investment climate has gained increased attention in recent years. Through the work of Hernando de Soto and others, the benefits of improved recognition and enforcement of the property rights associated with poor people's "invisible" assets (for example, untitled land) have received greater attention. The basic idea is that the establishment of a formal system for clearly and fairly recording and enforcing property rights, including rights held by the poor in a traditionally informal manner, can have a very strong positive effect on development. It will give the poor greater confidence in the security of their ownership rights to their property and as such better incentives to make longer-term investments. It may even go further, to the extent that it allows individuals or communities to use their property as security for leveraging additional financial resources that can be used for entrepreneurial activities or to expand or increase the productivity of existing enterprises (or agricultural activities).[24] The strengthening of property rights supports economic activity in other ways, such as by facilitating more efficient property transfers, the use of insurance, and joint ventures. Rule of Law projects administered by the World Bank, the USAID, and other development institutions are supporting work on this agenda.

Securing property rights is of great importance to the poor in developing countries who typically operate outside of formal property systems; who, as a result, lack the benefits of clear property rights noted above; and who live at risk of expropriation of their assets by the government or other actors. Further, large numbers of the poor are subsistence agriculturists who could realize substantial gains in productivity by investing in on-farm improvements, better seeds, fertilizer, and so on. The strong positive impact of microfinance initiatives such as the Grameen Bank also show how valuable the extension of credit to the poor, and poor women in particular, can be for starting small businesses.

The impact of governance quality on property rights is also well established. De Soto himself has pointed to the prevalence of corrupt, inefficient, and nontransparent government bureaucracies as one of the primary obstacles to the operation of private property in developing countries, and in his writings he offers several examples of the extensive procedural labyrinths that individuals must navigate before having a property right recognized. The World Bank tracks the difficulty of registering property in its Doing Business metric, and in doing so it has collected ample evidence of how poor governance undermines the functioning of private property. As the *Doing Business in 2006* report explained: "It takes 363 days to register property in Bangladesh, but only 1 in Norway and 2 in Sweden. The procedure costs around 21 percent of the property value in Chad, the Republic of Congo and Zimbabwe, but only 0.1 percent in Slovakia and New Zealand."[25] There is also empirical evidence that bureaucrats are likely to seek larger bribes from those who are dealing with the bureaucracy for the first time (for example, when registering property, including registering property as a first step to starting a formal business).[26] In summary, low levels of governance quality make registering property extremely difficult, and as a result, many individuals, particularly the poor, who are often least able to grapple with these difficulties, forgo property registration. As a result, they do not obtain the substantial benefits that de Soto and others have associated with property ownership.

Linkages through Public Services

After investment climate, the second factor on which development depends is human development, reflecting the reality that growth alone is not enough to reduce poverty quickly. "Investing in people" (that is, supporting human development) requires that good public services be effectively delivered.[27] A broad definition of public services is needed here, one which includes not only education, health, safe water, sanitation, urban development, roads and other transport infrastructure, and social safety nets, but also institutions whose rules, policies, and practices create and protect opportunities for individuals to develop and utilize their talents and skills. In this very broad sense, public services are to the human dimension of development what investment climate is to the economic dimension.

As with investment climate, better governance helps make services more responsive to a population's needs and preferences, and better governance diminishes the extent to which resources are siphoned off for other purposes or otherwise wasted.[28] To begin with, the data show that increased government spending on public services frequently does not result in better service delivery outcomes, such as health and education outcomes.[29] This disparity is largely due to poor governance, particularly institutional inefficiencies that could be addressed by improved transparency and accountability.[30] The soundness of allocative decisions also has a major impact on whether development goals are achieved. Too often governments direct scarce public resources to politically well-connected elites, rather than targeting resources to the greatest needs on the basis of some objective standard. Building transparency and accountability into budget processes and other public expenditure management processes can go a long way to improving allocative efficiency.[31] Additionally, as with investment climate, increased transparency and accountability can play a significant role in improving public services by reducing corruption—although studies vary with regard to how significant corruption is to the overall quality of public services.[32]

Do Outlier Countries Undermine the Case?

The existence of *outlier* countries, those countries that appear to demonstrate relatively strong economic performance in the face of relatively poor governance, poses a challenge to the idea that development actors should make improving transparency and accountability a priority. China is not high on many lists of "who does best" in terms of attributes like transparency and accountability, but its economic development over the last ten to twenty years has been unparalleled. Similarly, Chile far outstripped its neighbors in Latin America in reducing poverty and unemployment from the early 1980s through 1990 despite being under the autocratic control of the Pinochet military regime. Another example, Bangladesh, has recently enjoyed both social and economic development even while largely failing to improve relatively weak standards of governance.

One explanation for these cases—and more generally for other complexities in the country-by-country evidence—is that development is the result of many factors. A country that gets a strong positive development push from some factors may be able to more than compensate for a negative limitation from another factor. That is even more the case when one factor, as may be the case for indicators of governance quality, does not drive development as strongly as some other factors do. If this argument is correct, then China's development might have advanced even more briskly if its governance had been better. Of course, it is difficult to test this explanation, as it requires speculating as to how changes in already complex and in some respects nebulous attributes would have influenced economic and social development. Nonetheless, some observers point out that China's modern reform period started when the economy was at a very low level of productivity indeed, and it has grown thus far from low-income into the lower ranks of medium-income status. It remains to be seen how well China's current institutional arrangements, including weaknesses on some dimensions of governance, will serve the country as it rises further into the ranks of middle-income countries and strives to compete in increasingly complex economic activities.

China is rated in the lowest 10th percentile for voice and accountability but scores above the 50th percentile in government effectiveness and some aspects of anticorruption.[33] Further, its strong economic development since the government decided to switch from central planning to a market economy has been accompanied by major government reforms. Assessments of these reforms have concluded that they have been very successful in many ways (for example, in banking sector reform and in civil service reform), and this improvement in the country's governance deserves substantial credit for the country's accelerated development, although problems remain.[34] Additionally, despite the fact that transparency remains low in many respects, there is evidence that internal accountability has increased, as have external accountability pressures related to China's integration into the global economy and its accession to the World Trade Organization.

In the case of Chile, a closer analysis also reveals a more complex dynamic. First, Chile's "economic miracle" came on the heels of many years of relatively disappointing economic performance in the country, compounded by a near collapse during the Allende years, not to mention the larger economic downturn among many non-oil-exporting developing countries that was associated with the oil shocks and debt crisis of the late 1970s and early 1980s. As a result, some of the strong progress seen in Chile from the mid-1980s through early 1990s reflected a recovery to economic levels that Chile might have achieved earlier had it not been for multiple shocks, both external and self-inflicted. Second, foreign aid from the United States and Europe, including official aid and other forms of support (for example, increased market access) increased substantially following Allende's overthrow.[35] Third, in spite of the authoritarian and at times arbitrary exercise of power at the top under Pinochet, Chile continued to benefit from possessing some of the strongest public institutions in the region. Finally, although the trends of many economic indicators such as GDP growth were positive during the period of the "miracle," there is also little question not only that economic progress came with considerable social costs but also that a substantial part of the benefits of economic growth was captured by the already wealthy.[36]

Bangladesh offers a further set of questions. An assessment by the World Bank in 2005 concluded that the generally strong GDP growth rate since 1990 and the social gains (in literacy and nutrition, for example) occurred in the face of relatively stagnant and poor standards of governance during that time.[37] However, there is also evidence that a significant part of the country's progress can be credited to the efforts of civil society actors, including NGOs and microcredit providers like the Grameen Bank and Bangladesh Relief

Assistance Committee.[38] In other words, civil society actors seem to have been able to address some aspects of the country's development by essentially making an end run around a poorly performing government.

These examples show, not surprisingly, that the basic governance-development correlation does not tell the whole story of how and why some countries develop more rapidly than others. A closer analysis of these outliers, however, also shows that these countries do not undermine the idea that improved governance has a strong positive effect on development. In sum, there is an important causal correlation that merits attention, even if there are other factors of importance as well.

Notes

1. Deepa Narayan, with others, *Voices of the Poor: Can Anyone Hear Us?* (Published for the World Bank by Oxford University Press, 2000), p. 32.

2. Amartya Sen, *Poverty and Famines: An Essay on Entitlements and Deprivation* (Oxford, United Kingdom: Clarendon Press, 1982).

3. Daniel Kaufmann, Aart Kraay, and Massimo Mastruzzi, "The Worldwide Governance Indicators Project: Answering the Critics" (Washington: World Bank, February 2007).

4. World Bank, "A Decade of Measuring the Quality of Governance" (Washington, 2006).

5. Daniel Kaufmann and Aart Kraay, "Growth without Governance," *Economía* 3, no. 1 (Fall 2002): 169–229.

6. See, for example, Robert E. Hall and Charles Jones, "Why Do Some Countries Produce So Much More Output per Worker than Others?" *Quarterly Journal of Economics* 114, no. 1 (1999): 83–116; Daron Acemoglu, Simon Johnson, and James A. Robinson, "Colonial Origins of Comparative Development: An Empirical Investigation," *American Economic Review* 91, no. 5 (2001): 1369–401; William Easterly and Ross Levine, "Tropics, Germs, and Crops: How Endowments Influence Economic Development," Carnegie-Rochester Conference Series on Public Policy, "Economic Growth and the Role of Institutions" (Simon School, University of Rochester, New York, April 19–20, 2002).

7. See, for example, Hall and Jones, "Why Do Some Countries Produce So Much More Output?"; Kaufmann and Kraay, "Growth without Governance."

8. Daniel Kaufmann, Aart Kraay, and Massimo Mastruzzi, *Governance Matters IV: Governance Indicators for 1996–2004* (Washington: World Bank, 2005), p. 37; World Bank, *Global Monitoring Report 2006* (Washington, 2006), p. 122.

9. Daniel Kaufmann, "Human Rights, Governance and Development: An Empirical Perspective," *Development Outreach* (January 2007).

10. Daniel Kaufmann, "Myths and Realities of Governance and Corruption" (Washington: World Bank: September 2005), pp. 96–97.

11. See, for example, the lists of factors cited in high-level international development declarations, such as the "2005 World Summit Report," Document A/60/L.1 (United Nations General Assembly, September 20, 2005), or the "United Nations Millennium Declaration," ResolutionA/RES/55/2 (United Nations General Assembly, September 18, 2000).

12. See summaries in the World Bank's series of *World Development Reports.*

13. World Bank, *World Development Report 2005: A Better Investment Climate for Everyone* (Washington, 2005).

14. World Bank, *Doing Business in 2005: Removing Obstacles to Growth* (Washington, 2004); Douglass North, *Institutions, Institutional Change and Economic Performance* (Cambridge University Press, 1990); Robin Burgess and Tony Venables, "Towards a Microeconomics of Growth" (London School of Economics, 2003).

15. Geeta Batra, Daniel Kaufmann, and Andrew H. W. Stone, *Investment Climate around the World: Voices of the Firms from the World Business Environment Survey* (Washington: World Bank, 2003); World Bank, "An Evaluation of World Bank Investment Climate Activities" (Washington: World Bank, 2004), p. 3.

16. See chapter 4 for a discussion of the various ways in which government entities can be held accountable.

17. R. M. Desai and S. Pradhan, "Governing the Investment Climate," *Development Outreach* (March 2005), p. 2.

18. Warrick Smith and Mary Hallward-Driemeier, "Understanding the Investment Climate," *Finance and Development* (March 2005), p. 41.

19. Smith and Hallward-Driemeier, "Understanding the Investment Climate."

20. Paulo Mauro, "Corruption and Growth," *Quarterly Journal of Economics* 110, no. 3 (August 1995): 681–712.

21. Stephen Knack and Philip Keefer, "Institutions and Economic Performance: Cross-Country Tests Using Alternative Institutional Measures," *Economics and Politics* 7, no. 3 (1995): 207–28.

22. Simeon Djankov and others, "The Regulation of Entry," *Quarterly Journal of Economics* 117, no. 1 (February 2002): 1–37. A side payment may often be a direct bribe but might possibly be a payment to an "expediter" who may either pay a bribe in turn or possibly spend the time sitting in lines that the business owner would rather not do.

23. World Bank, *Doing Business in 2007—How to Reform* (Washington, 2006).

24. Hernando de Soto, *The Mystery of Capital: Why Capitalism Triumphs in the West and Fails Everywhere Else* (New York: Basic Books, 2000).

25. World Bank, *Doing Business in 2006: Creating Jobs* (Washington, 2006), p. 27.

26. George Clarke and Lixin Xu, "Ownership, Competition and Corruption: Bribe Takers versus Bribe Payers," Policy Research Working Paper 2783 (Washington: World Bank, February 2002).

27. World Bank, *World Development Report 2004: Making Services Work for Poor People* (Washington, 2004).

28. Elia Armstrong, "Integrity, Transparency and Accountability in Public Administration: Recent Trends, Regional and International Developments and Emerging

Issues," Discussion Paper (United Nations, Department of Economic and Social Affairs, August 2005), pp. 2–3.

29. World Bank, *World Development Report 2004,* p. 37.

30. See, for example, Andrew Sunil Rajkumar and Vinaya Swaroop, "Public Spending and Outcomes: Does Governance Matter?" Policy Research Working Paper 2840 (Washington: World Bank, May 7, 2002).

31. See, example, International Budget Project, "Can Civil Society Add Value to Budget Decision-Making?" (Washington, 2005).

32. For examples of studies finding evidence of a linkage, see Rajkumar and Swaroop, "Public Spending and Outcomes"; Sanjeev Gupta, Marijn Verhoeven, and Erwin R. Tiongson, "The Effectiveness of Government Spending on Education and Health Care in Developing and Transition Economics," *European Journal of Political Economy* 18, no. 4 (2002): 717–37. For a study finding the contrary, see Ruwan Jayasuriya and Quentin Wodon, "Explaining Country Efficiency in Improving Health and Education Indicators: The Role of Urbanization" (Washington: World Bank, 2002).

33. Daniel Kaufmann, Aart Kraay, and Massimo Mastruzzi, *Governance Matters V: Governance Indicators for 1996–2005* (Washington: World Bank, 2006).

34. Asian Development Bank, *Development Management: Progress and Challenges in the PRC* (Manila, 2002), chapter 3.

35. J. Petras and S. Vieux, "The Chilean 'Economic Miracle': An Empirical Critique," *Critical Sociology* 17, no. 2 (1990): 57–72.

36. J. Schatan, "The Deceitful Nature of Socio-Economic Indicators," *Development* 3–4 (1990): 69–75.

37. World Bank, "Bangladesh—Country Brief" (Washington, July 2005).

38. M. Jahangir and Alam Chowdhury, "The Impact of Micro-Credit on Poverty: Evidence from Bangladesh," *Progress in Development Studies* 5, no. 4 (2005): 298–309.

The Response

PART

II

3

Overview

Part I concluded that improved governance matters to countries, in part because it is linked to improved development outcomes. But what determines why one country has better governance than another? And how can groups within a country, or sympathetic outside actors, help to improve those standards?

These questions provide the context for this and the following chapters. Among other goals, this discussion seeks to respond to the call—by the African minister cited at the outset of chapter 1 and by many others—for an integrated analytical framework to help understand what influences standards of accountability, transparency, and governance across different countries.

The framework presented here should be of interest to those who wish to analyze governance standards in different countries. But this is not its only, or indeed its primary, objective. The analysis can also be of practical assistance to those whose objective is to try to raise standards of governance and accountability at the country level. These actors might, for example, be aspiring reformers within government or politics; actors in civil society, such as homegrown NGOs, who may have the potential to help hold government agencies to account; or international organizations, such as foundations, NGOs, or multilateral agencies, who seek to support domestic efforts at improving the quality of government performance.

This chapter provides a succinct preview of the framework that will be presented over chapters 4 to 9, each of which focuses on a particular part of the puzzle. Several of the chapters present analytical models drawn from social science research, each of which is intended to help illuminate some dimension of the larger story.

Crucial to the overall framework is the concept that the effectiveness, integrity, and accountability of government in any particular country are influenced by a series of interactions between different elements in the society—ordinary citizens, businesses, civil society organizations (CSOs) such as religious groups or NGOs, the media, and so on—and those within government, including politicians and civil servants. The various groups outside government pose multiple demands on those within government—some may be asking for special favors for themselves, and others may be asking for government services that are honest, efficient, and equitable. Those in government may respond positively to some of these demands, while ignoring or actively resisting others. To apply the terminology of the model that will be presented in chapter 6, the different elements in society and government exchange "signals and actions."

Outline of the Book

In chapter 4, the focus is on the implications of *principal-agent models* for governance. These models were originally developed to illuminate the challenge for owners of firms (*principals*) in trying to ensure that their managers (*agents*) acted in line with the owners' interests rather than purely following the personal interests of the managers themselves. But principal-agent models can also help illuminate the relationship between citizen-voters (viewed as principals) and the politicians and bureaucrats within government (who may be viewed as their agents). Just as the owners of a firm expect their managers to act in the owners' interests, so the citizens would hope to see their own agents acting in the citizens' interests, rather than in the interests of the politicians and officials themselves. Among the potentially relevant insights from this model are the different channels for principals to create incentives that will influence agents' behavior so as to align it with the principals' interests, including mechanisms for recruiting (and dismissing) agents, the design of incentive systems for agents (carrots and sticks), and the importance of efforts to observe agents' behavior. In government systems, specifically, channels for holding officials accountable may operate from top down (as in effective hierarchies), from sideways (including professional peer pressure), or from bottom up (by or on behalf of the general public).

A particular challenge is raised by the *collective action problem*, which indicates that a relatively small group of players, each of whom has a great deal at stake in any particular decision, is more likely to organize effectively to influence the outcome than a much larger group of actors, each of whom individually has only a modest amount at stake. The implication is that vested interests may often carry more weight in decisions that directly affect them than will a concern for the interests of the general public. This does not necessarily make it impossible for the interests of the general public to be heard, but it does raise the stakes for those trying to organize effective intermediary institutions to represent the interests of ordinary citizens on these occasions.

Interest group dynamics are the focus of chapter 5. The principal-agent model, however useful its insights, represents a simplification of reality. Society is not, in fact, made up of a homogeneous group of like-minded and public-spirited citizen-principals. Rather, we witness perpetual maneuvering by myriad special interests to secure advantages for themselves or, in the case of intermediary organizations, for those they represent. Classic pluralist models emphasize the importance of freedom of organization and lobbying for all, so that every voice has a chance to be heard. Corporatist models, by contrast, emphasize that governments are liable to be influenced most by those special interests that can most effectively amass and effectively use power to skew decisions in their favor.

Signals and actions are explored further in chapter 6. Signal theory explores some of the issues that arise whenever one group of people seeks to influence the behavior of another, for example, as in the case of a civil society organization that seeks to convey the demand for greater transparency or equity in the use of public resources. The messages that the CSO seeks to convey are known in this approach as signals. The signal approach highlights such aspects as the effectiveness of the formulation of a signal and of its transmission to those it is intended to reach, as well as its efficient (or less than efficient) reception by its target audience. In turn, questions arise about the formulation of any response (action), and possible feedback or backlash to that response. For instance, if citizens are hindered in how they can communicate effectively with decisionmakers at the top (for example, elections are not fair), or if leaders have impunity (they can ignore citizens' messages because, for example, they are immune from being removed or otherwise sanctioned), then the effectiveness of the signals and the prospects for achieving good outcomes are curtailed correspondingly, just as impedance (signal loss) interferes with electrical circuits.

Crucial to any country-specific discussion of the relationship between the public and civil society groups and those in government is the nature of the *political system,* which is the focus of chapter 7. To choose extreme examples, the potential for ordinary citizens to influence any aspect of public sector performance will clearly differ greatly depending on whether one is considering a functioning democracy, with competitive elections, respect for the rule of law, and a free press, or an autocratic regime in which any criticism of the government is liable to land the critic in jail. In between these extremes, of course, are multiple shades of gray, and the chapter considers different ways of classifying country systems, including the fact that regimes may evolve over time. The extent and nature of democracy, institutionalization, executive power, citizen voice, authoritarianism, and related attributes of a society's political arrangements have an influence on, and are influenced by, the interactions among key actors and the outcomes of those interactions.

Chapter 8 focuses on *interventions,* by which we mean the deliberate measures that actors take to try to remedy problems in how the process outlined here is working. These interventions can include, for example, the strengthening of independent watchdog organizations that press for better government performance. Or the interventions might focus instead on getting the vote to disenfranchised groups.

Chapter 9 discusses some of the challenges that likely arise in trying to apply the analytical framework discussed here at the level of an *individual country analysis.*

Finally, the appendixes are composed of a series of country case studies of selected aspects of accountability in diverse country settings, with a special emphasis on the crucial question of how government spending is managed at the country level.

Each of these building blocks for the framework is developed further below. The resulting framework is, in part, a fusing together of the principal-agent model and the interest-group-dynamics model. Other approaches have focused on one aspect of the whole (on transparency or corruption alone but not both together, for instance); the intent here is to complement those efforts with an analytical framework for examining multiple aspects together—transparency, accountability, governance, and anticorruption.

That said, the logic of the argument here leads naturally to increased attention to the accountability dimension of the story. In effect, the framework offers insights on the mechanics of how accountability forces operate upon governments (the principal-agent dynamic), while also accounting for underlying political economy considerations (the special interest group dynamic). The concepts of signals and actions explore the pathways by which citizens and other actors attempt to hold governments accountable. The resulting analytical framework offers an approach that is more process oriented than previous studies of individual components of good governance have been. Because of that, this framework provides an entry point to mapping out and analyzing the processes by which governments are held accountable in individual country contexts.

4 | *Principals and Agents*

A principal-agent relationship, according to the standard theory, is an arrangement under which one actor, referred to as the *agent,* is charged with performing certain acts that are useful to another actor, called the *principal,* typically in exchange for compensation from the principal. This basic model, while originally developed in a business management context, has subsequently been widely used to illuminate the interactions between citizens and their government.[1]

The Basic Model: Principals and Agents in Business

The original relationship modeled by the principal-agent theory is that of the owner or owners of a firm who hire a manager or managers to run their firm. The owners will have certain goals and expectations about the way they want their firm operated. In simplified terms, they may want their own paid-out profits to be maximized. However, there may be more to their goals than this. The owners very likely will want the managers to adopt a long-term rather than a short-term approach to maximizing profits, so as to safeguard the value of the owners' equity in the firm. They may well have certain expectations as to how much risk they want the firm to take on: too much caution and the firm may ossify; too much risk and the firm may fall into bankruptcy. They might also have expectations of a nonprofit nature as well: perhaps certain goals of social responsibility or good environmental stewardship.

The principal-agent problem arises to the extent that the agent's interests differ substantially from the principal's, that the principal cannot easily observe the agent's performance, that the principal cannot compel the agent to behave in accordance with the principal's interests, or some combination of these.[2] There are multiple ways in which the agent's perceived self-interest might diverge from that of the principal(s). The agent might, for example, seek to maximize his or her own emoluments (or leisure) or favor friends or relatives in contracts made on behalf of the company. The agent might take on more or less risk than the principal would wish or flout the principals' social values.

The theory directs our attention to various complementary approaches the principal can adopt in trying to ensure that the agent acts as closely as possible in line with the principal's wishes and interests.

Recruitment

Principals will try to select agents who are then expected to act in the principal's best interests. For one thing, they will certainly try to hire agents who provide evidence that suggests that they possess competence (for example, prior successful experience in business or a résumé that shows knowledge and experience in other fields such as academic life or the military). But they may also be concerned about finding agents who share their own values, by choosing a member of their own social or religious group, for example.

Policy and Incentive Structure

Principals will typically try to design systems of rules, contracts, and incentive systems calculated to align the agent's interests with their own. A common approach is to tie a significant portion of the agent's compensation to the level of profits earned by the firm. However, if agents are compensated largely on the basis of short-term profits, they may be tempted to neglect the long-term future of the firm and take higher risks in the pursuit of high, immediate profits than the principal would wish. The perception that some Wall Street firms may have followed this course over recent years is behind discussions of requiring senior managers and traders to take a higher proportion of their total compensation on a deferred basis—which is dependent on the medium-term progress of the firm rather than on its immediate annual earnings. Beyond the question of the performance indicators for agents, principals can also use the threat of dismissal to deter behavior of which they disapprove.

Observation of Agent's Behavior as a Basis for Corrective Action by the Principal

Principals need accurate, relevant, and timely information on what their agents are doing. That way, if the agent is going in the wrong direction, the principals have some hope of being able to take corrective actions before too much damage is done. Two broad questions arise: what should be observed and who should observe it? These questions continue to be controversial in the business world today. Commentators debate, for example, whether firms' accounts, which are used as the basic device for tracking management performance, should always be "marked to market" to take account of variations in the market valuations of the firm's assets. There is also active discussion over the role of the board of directors, which is generally expected to serve as a key representative of the shareholders in monitoring the performance of managers. How should directors be selected? Should the board chairman be independent of management? A number of recent spectacular business failures, such as that of press baron Lord (Conrad) Black, are widely attributed to the failure of the relevant board to exercise sufficient independence in its monitoring of management.

Applying the Principal-Agent Model to Politics and Government

Many observers have noted the potential relevance of the principal-agent model to the relationship between citizens and their governments. In this approach, citizens, whether defined as the general public, voters, service users, or taxpayers, are viewed as the principals. The agents are the government, whether understood as a whole, as specific units of the state, or as individual officials. This application of the model embodies the assumption that the legitimacy and power of a government ultimately derive from those it governs and that a government's primary purpose is to serve the interests of the electorate. Analysis based on the principal-agent model brings attention to how far, and by what mechanisms, the general population can enforce or encourage desired behavior on the part of its agents in government.

Figure 4-1 offers a basic graphical presentation of the principal-agent model applied to a government context. The first step (A) is the selection of the agent. The second step (B) is the design and ongoing adjustment of the policy and institutional environment (including the incentive framework) within which the agents operate. The third step (C) involves efforts to observe the agent's behavior. The fourth step (D) deals with how identified problems can be addressed.

Hiring (and Firing) the Agent

As discussed earlier, a key step in any principal-agent relationship is the selection of the agent. Since the mechanisms for hiring a new agent are often

Figure 4-1. *Basic Structure of the Principal-Agent Model of Government Accountability*

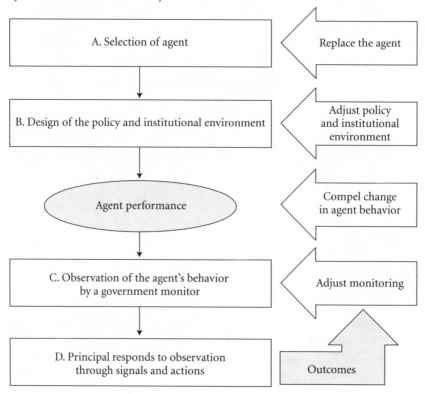

closely related to those for firing an agent viewed as unsatisfactory, it makes sense to discuss the two stages together.

Agent selection in the sphere of government inevitably takes place at multiple levels and in a variety of ways. Typically, in political systems with some element of popular elections, the electoral process will be used periodically to choose one or more than one senior political figure. These elected politicians then become responsible for selecting and holding accountable lower-level political appointees and for supervising and holding accountable (if generally not for selecting) career civil servants.

The directly elected figures will typically include the president in a presidential system, as well as members of the legislative branch (congress or parliament). In a purely parliamentary system, the support of a majority of the members of parliament provides the basis for forming an administration to operate the executive branch. Local governments, likewise, are in many countries led by directly elected figures in positions such as governors, mayors, and councilors.

Role of Elections

Elections provide a direct mechanism for the general adult population, in the role of principal, to try to select leaders who—on the basis of its assessment of the candidates' promises, experience, and values—the electorate hopes will serve as effective agents. Correspondingly, elections represent the population's ultimate method for sanctioning agents they believe have failed them.

What determines the efficiency of elections as a mechanism for promoting accountability? One important element is the degree of competitiveness of the contest. Do opposition parties face unreasonable procedural hurdles? Does the incumbent administration largely dominate the communications media? A number of groups around the world, which have experience in providing independent election observers, have worked out a significant degree of consensus in what constitute "free and fair" elections.

But beyond possible manipulation of the polls or domination of the airwaves, there are other factors that affect the effectiveness of elections specifically as a mechanism for selecting agents and holding them accountable. How much information do electors receive about the different candidates? Do the different parties set out clear manifestos of their policy commitments? How do the voters react to the information available to them? How educated are the voters? Are they disposed to make their choices based on a party's record in power or are they more inclined to vote on the basis of communal factors such as a candidate's religion or ethnic identity?

Hiring (and Firing) Nonelected Officials

Systems differ significantly across countries as to the proportion of the executive branch officials who are *political appointees,* that is to say, officials who are hired (and potentially fired) by the administration of the day on the basis of political considerations vis-à-vis officials who are *career civil servants* and who, as such, are hired according to technocratic criteria, serve under governments of different political ideologies, and enjoy significant security of tenure. When Gordon Brown became British prime minister in July 2007, for example, he announced a government made up of 133 political appointees, including ministers, deputy ministers, parliamentary secretaries, and the like.[3] Within each ministry in the United Kingdom, the overwhelming proportion of officials will be career civil servants, reporting ultimately to about half a dozen political appointees per ministry. The United States administration, by contrast, was estimated in 2006 to include more than 2,786 political appointees.[4]

Systems for holding officials accountable (including promotions and dismissals) tend to vary primarily depending on whether they are political or career appointees. A political appointee typically serves at the pleasure of the elected official who originally made the appointment. Accountability in this case is political accountability—when the lower-level official becomes a political embarrassment or just "in the way," his or her scalp is demanded and received. Career civil servants, by contrast, are more likely to be covered by elaborate apolitical systems for evaluation, promotion, and dismissal—the latter typically done only in cases of clear misconduct, although bureaucracies find their own ways of moving those perceived as weak performers or troublemakers into marginal posts.

There is some evidence in the literature that government entities that employ open, merit-based systems may typically perform substantially better than those in which political patronage determines appointments.[5] Another significant factor highlighted in the literature is the extent to which government employee unions influence the selection process, particularly in regard to the rules for removing ineffective officials.[6] In Mexico, for example, teachers in the public schools owe their positions to the teachers' union rather than to the government or school principals, and this situation has posed a major challenge to efforts to improve accountability and learning in a system that ranks last out of all Organization for Economic Cooperation and Development member countries on standardized tests of student achievement.[7]

Contracting Procedures for Private Sector Suppliers

Privatization and public-private partnerships increasingly play a role in the delivery of public services, and this makes the procedures used to award contracts an important element in achieving efficient delivery of public services. Although there are varying processes by which private sector firms can enter into arrangements to provide public services, the contracting of firms typically follows a procedure whereby the government issues a request for bids from prospective service providers, then reviews submitted bids, and finally enters into an agreement with the successful bidder. The transparency of the competitive process and the criteria used to select the winning bidder are important elements in determining how compatible these processes are with the achievement of good governance.

Policy and Institutional Environment

The earlier discussion of the principal-agent model in the business sector pointed to the importance of the incentive framework facing managers engaged by the owners of a firm. What is the equivalent framework when the model is applied to a government?

Any government entity (understood as either an individual official or a larger governmental unit) works within a policy and institutional environment that, if well designed, maintained, and adjusted, can increase accountability and improve governance. Crucial among the incentives, as seen already, is the potential for at least the top political members of the administration to be thrown out of office if their performance does not satisfy the electorate.

There are, in addition, many other factors that may affect the incentive climate for the entire public sector. Among other things, an assessment of the policy and institutional environment might include a review of the following:

—The entity's responsibilities, including the powers that the entity can assert and those which it is precluded from claiming

—The resources and support (including training) that is provided to enable the entity to complete its duties

—Any incentives in place for effective performance

—Official controls intended to ensure that the entity functions appropriately in terms of honesty and efficiency

An assessment of the entity's responsibilities is typically specific to the particular government entity targeted. It is important to understand where decisions are actually made in practice, particularly in cases in which monitoring efforts target a decentralized government entity, since central governments may retain far more control over decentralized functions than may be formally indicated.

Resources and support are more amenable than an entity's responsibilities to a standardized analysis. Particularly important are management policies and practices concerning public expenditures, which may represent a critical determinant of how far governments meet the needs of their citizens. This includes high-level budgeting processes as well as the processes by which ministries make allocative decisions, including either reallocations or allocations within a more general funding window approved by the executive or parliament or both. Understanding how the targeted entity receives its funding provides crucial insights into several aspects of accountability.

First, a review of the entity's funding will go a long way toward revealing whether it has adequate resources to deliver sufficient goods and services to the public, such as education, health care, or food for the poor, or to effectively execute other administrative and regulatory functions. This may in turn influence decisions by monitoring organizations on how and when to engage with the management process for public expenditures, with a view to pushing for additional funding for underresourced programs or, alternatively, for reallocations from low-priority to high-priority programs.

A second question is how far budgetary allocations to different government agencies are linked to performance measures. Budgeting procedures in much of the world, especially in developing countries, make disappointingly limited use of performance-based budgeting, which could potentially make a substantial impact in heightening the public sector's focus on effective performance. Beyond financial flows, other forms of resources may also be highly relevant, such as the supply of trained and experienced staff to different agencies within the overall public sector. Seeing which parts of the public service get the most highly rated recruits can tell an analyst something important about an administration's true priorities.[8]

In principle, incentives may be positive or negative in nature, that is to say, the carrot or the stick. Some of these implicit incentives have already been discussed: the risk of loss of political office because of electoral failure, the risk of relegation to a marginal position for any official, and the bases upon which resources of money and manpower are allocated between agencies. The remuneration of individual civil servants may sometimes include a modest element of performance-related pay, but in general other factors, such as seniority, have usually tended to play a more important role.

Controls include auditors, inspectors general, ombudsmen, anticorruption bodies, and law enforcement officers, as well as institutional policies and processes for functions such as elections, access to information, disclosure of information, and public consultations. Table 4-1 lists several of these entities, as well as the potential accountability functions associated with them and some of the common obstacles to fulfillment of those functions.

Observing the Agent's Behavior

As in our earlier discussion of the principal-agent model, for accountability to work, it is crucial that there be effective systems for observing the agent's behavior. As before, the two basic questions are: what should be observed and who should observe it?

What Information Should Be Observed?

The information that it is most relevant to observe will depend heavily on who the would-be observer is and what the observer's objectives are. Political

Table 4-1. *Definitions, Initiatives, Actors, and Programs*

Control mechanism	Potential governance functions	Typical shortcomings
Auditors, inspectors general, ombudsmen, anticorruption bodies, and other law enforcement officials	Review government actions Investigate claims of misuse of resources Provide data and analysis for other actors	Lack of independence Inadequate resources Limited jurisdiction Limited information access Lack of a mandate or capability for performance audits
Electoral processes and institutions	Primary mechanism for controlling governments through selection and removal of regimes and individual politicians Threat of electoral punishment deters bad behavior Desire for reelection serves as incentive for good performance	Infrequent elections Unfair elections Lack of political competition Voting not based on government's performance (but on identity issues, for example) Votes bought through patronage or party machines rather than earned by performance
Information access policies	Allow government monitors to obtain data on government performance Discourage bad behavior because of risk that it will subsequently be uncovered (and punished)	Policies have too many exceptions Policies provide officials with excessive discretion No detailed records Lack of mechanisms for enforcing policies
Disclosure policies	Require government to make information on its actions available to the public Discourage bad behavior if officials must publicize decisions	Policies have too many exceptions Policies provide officials with excessive discretion Officials disclose insufficient information Officials disclose excessive raw data that are difficult for citizens to process Lack of mechanisms for enforcing policies
Consultation policies and mechanisms	Provide mechanism for government monitors and other public interest organizations to express concerns and suggest remedies to government	Lack of consultation Lack of response by government

leaders of a government, for example, will want to collect a wide range of information about the performance of those serving under them, including especially information relevant to any political risks or opportunities. By contrast, if one were to put oneself in the position of a public interest–oriented institution, such as an independent monitoring organization, the information that would be most relevant would relate primarily to the effectiveness of the public sector in the efficient and equitable delivery of services to the general population, perhaps with a special focus on the extent to which the more vulnerable groups are adequately reached.

Among the crucial issues that will arise in monitoring government expenditure and service delivery are the following:

—*Honesty.* Many discussions of accountability and governance focus almost exclusively on whether government officials are honest or corrupt. Although individual standards of integrity matter, a more serious problem exists when an entire institution (or the government as a whole) loses respect for professionalism and integrity, and corrupt behavior becomes the expected norm.

—*Effectiveness and efficiency.* Although honesty is important, it is also vital to observe whether government entities are performing effectively and efficiently. Are decisionmakers and service providers technically competent and is the entity using its resources efficiently? Do services and their delivery systems reflect an up-to-date understanding of the relevant technical alternatives? Are costs appropriately constrained and waste minimized?

—*Equity.* How does the delivery of public services compare between different parts of the population? Are there significant variations in the level of spending or the quality of services between urban and rural areas or across different regions of the country? Do particular ethnic, religious, or caste groups receive second-class treatment? Do more affluent residential areas benefit from better treatment? Do more affluent or better-educated couples find ways to get better public education for their children or better public health treatment for their parents?

—*Process and substance.* The type of information required can also be split between process-related and substantive information. The term *process-related* refers to information about the observed government entity's procedures and practices in regard to transparency and openness. That includes, for example, information on the laws and rules concerning disclosure and access to information, public consultation and input, and dispute resolution. The term *substantive information* refers to information on the actual allocations and delivery operations of the observed government entity.

—Forward and backward. A government monitor also needs to determine the direction of observation. Many monitoring efforts (audits are one example) are *backward looking,* in the sense that the information examined refers to past government performance. Monitoring may also need to be *forward looking.* For example, the monitor may need to assess the appropriateness of resource allocations made in budgets or strategic investment plans (and may need to do so while the budget or plan is still at a draft stage when it is still possible to make changes).

In addition to determining what type of information is needed, a government monitor must grapple with determining what information is actually accessible. In many developing countries, a lack of information and transparency on government performance can be the primary obstacle to accountability and good governance. Accordingly, government monitors may be limited in the immediate term to gaining access to the information that is available to them, while also working (perhaps in tandem with others) over the medium to longer term to increase access to information on government processes and performance.

There are, in turn, two dimensions to the issue of information availability. In one example, essential information is being collected and tabulated and made available to insiders but not to the general public or outside monitors. In this case, the recourse for civil society monitors will be to agitate, preferably in alliance with other groups in the society, for opening up access to information through freedom of information or sunshine laws.

All too often, though, much of the information needed for good substantive monitoring of the effectiveness, efficiency, and equity of public services may not be collected at all (or not assembled into formats that readily answer the key questions). Detailed studies of public expenditure systems in developing countries indicate that data are often only available with long lags and that customary classification systems conceal more than they reveal. Pressing for countries to adopt improved systems of public expenditure management may thus be a high priority for CSOs working in this area.

Who Observes the Agent?

The analytical framework presented in this book distinguishes among four types of accountability: top-down, sideways, bottom-up, and external, each of which may potentially play a significant role in holding a government unit accountable by monitoring its performance (see figure 4-2).[9]

Top-down accountability. Accountability operates to a greater or lesser degree *within* governments. In a functioning hierarchical system, those at the

Figure 4-2. *General Types of Accountability*

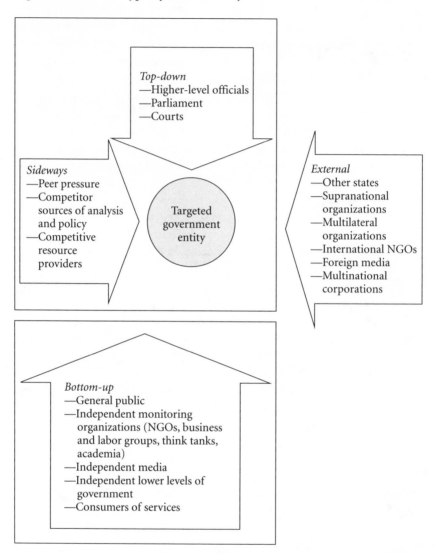

Top-down
—Higher-level officials
—Parliament
—Courts

Sideways
—Peer pressure
—Competitor
 sources of analysis
 and policy
—Competitive
 resource
 providers

Targeted
government
entity

External
—Other states
—Supranational
 organizations
—Multilateral
 organizations
—International NGOs
—Foreign media
—Multinational
 corporations

Bottom-up
—General public
—Independent monitoring
 organizations (NGOs, business
 and labor groups, think tanks,
 academia)
—Independent media
—Independent lower levels of
 government
—Consumers of services

top may be able to exercise a high degree of effective control over those further down in the system. Note that what we are talking about here is the ability of the leadership to impose its own goals, values, and objectives on the
bureaucracy. Depending on country circumstances, this may or may not
translate into enforcement of the standards of efficiency, equity, and transparency that we or a public interest organization may view as representing

Table 4-2. *Overview of Potential Top-Down Accountability Mechanisms*

Top-down actors	Potential accountability functions	Potential obstacles
Higher-level officials	Exercise general management and oversight authority	Weak oversight capacity
		Lack of instruments to effect change
		Lack of incentive
		Inadequate information or performance
Parliaments	Review government actions (through reporting requirements, hearings, and so forth)	Lack of independence
		Insufficient legislative authority
		Weak oversight capacity
	Legislate changes to policy and institutional environment	Limited information access
Courts and law enforcement entities	Review government actions	Lack of independence
	Provide forum for redress of corruption	Limited jurisdiction
	Issue orders to enjoin or force action	Lack of authority
		Insufficient technical expertise

good government. On the one hand, a powerful but corrupt central government may be comfortable allowing the continued misuse of public resources, because, for example, the abuser is part of larger system of patronage that helps the government maintain power or because incentives are inadequate to promote the effective use of resources (for example, there is little threat of political repercussions or no reward for improving performance). On the other hand, strong central governments in some countries are certainly capable of adopting an ethos that is strongly prodevelopment, as has happened in many of the East Asian states over recent decades. The case study of Thailand in appendix E, for example, presents a system in which senior officials in the core economic policy agencies have been largely insulated from day-to-day political pressures, which enables them to pursue economic stability and rapid (if not always equitably distributed) growth. Table 4-2 lists several entities that have express or implied top-down accountability functions.

Sideways accountability. Sideways accountability roughly translates into peer pressure, which can be particularly efficacious among professional service providers. One example of this type of accountability is found in academia. Many university professors, especially those with tenure, operate with little or no top-down (administrator) or bottom-up (student) control. Rather, the main source of accountability is other academics, particularly those in their field.

The extent to which this type of peer pressure exists, or could be enhanced, among public officials is less clear and is dependent on the particular subset of public officials. Higher-skilled professionals with specialized knowledge, such as accountants and physicians, generally are likely to be subject to significant peer pressure from their professional peers who operate outside the government and meet their government counterparts in the same professional associations, alumni organizations, and so forth. The development of strong peer pressure among generalist administrators is less of an automatic process, but it can be achieved, especially in systems largely managed by career civil servants as opposed to those dominated by political appointees. Many countries have consciously sought to develop an elite corps of high-flying administrators, as in India, for example.[10] Beyond this, in environments with vigorous civil society organizations and think tanks, where there is substantial disclosure of information by the government and analytical capabilities outside of government, significant peer pressure can be applied on mid- and upper-level bureaucrats as the policy process becomes more professionalized and knowledge based.[11]

Bottom-up accountability. The ultimate source of government accountability is the public. In an ideal system, the people are able to hold their government accountable because they can effectively monitor the government's performance and take action to address identified shortcomings. In practice, there are, of course, many challenges to effective bottom-up accountability, particularly in developing countries. Perhaps the most significant is the collective action problem, which makes it difficult for the public to act as a group.

The concept of a collective action problem, first formulated explicitly by Mancur Olson, is by now well established in the economic and social science literature.[12] Olson posits that those who have a great deal directly at stake in a particular government decision, often a relatively small number of players, will find it in their interests to incur the costs of organizing effectively to lobby for their shared interests, while the possibly much larger groups of those with competing interests, each of whom individually has only a small amount at stake, may not even recognize their interests and are in any case less likely to find it worth their while to organize in their own collective interests. Typical examples of the collective action problem involve struggles over trade protection or subsidies for a specific industry or sector. The businesses and labor unions in the sector under consideration for a subsidy are likely to work hard to obtain or retain their special treatment. The general public, whether as consumers paying a bit more for the product from the protected industry or as taxpayers footing the bill for one more subsidy, is much less likely to find it worthwhile to work hard to defeat the favor to a particular industry.

In the present context, the collective action model is applied to the situation of citizens as a whole (or to a large subset of the population, such as users of various public services) who have a strong interest in improving the quality of government performance but who are not well organized and do not function effectively as a unit. At the level of an individual, as Olson's model implies, the cost of acting alone to monitor agents and hold them accountable may well be astronomical, and this cost to the individual will far outweigh any benefits that the individual could capture.

The problem need not lead to despair, however. Independent monitoring organizations, such as community groups, NGOs, research and policy organizations, faith-based groups, business associations, public commissions, and oversight boards, can serve as instruments that enable segments of the general public to overcome the collective action problem to enforce their interests. In this model, at least some members of the collective—or professional organizers acting on their behalf—recognize the shared interest that exists and the need for accountability, and so they either form independent monitoring organizations themselves or provide resources to support such organizations that then act as their proxies. While many individuals will either not recognize their interest in supporting such an effort or will choose to act as "free riders" who allow others to incur the costs of action, the proliferation of community groups and NGOs in recent years suggests that this can be a viable method of increasing accountability.

In addition to the types of independent monitoring organizations discussed above, other channels for promoting accountability operate in most societies. These include independent news media (radio, television, newsprint, and Internet journalists and publishers), private businesses, academic entities (individual academics and their institutions), and even lower-level government units (if they have a degree of independence from the national government). Table 4-3 provides an overview of the various actors that can contribute to bottom-up accountability and some of the potential obstacles to their playing that role effectively.

External accountability. The three above-mentioned types of accountability originate within a country. Of course, countries are not closed boxes, and external actors may also play a role in holding governments accountable for their actions. These actors include other nation-states (particularly neighbors,

Table 4-3. *Overview of Potential Bottom-Up Accountability Mechanisms*

Bottom-up actors	Potential accountability functions	Potential obstacles
Direct action by general public	Provides threat of government replacement to motivate better performance Puts pressure on decisionmakers and service providers	Collective action problem Lack of information access Limited technical expertise
The media	Disseminate information to the public Disseminate information to decisionmakers Conduct investigative reporting	Lack of independence Limited readership and audience Lack of credibility with public Lack of credibility with decisionmakers Insufficient access to information Limited technical expertise
Research and policy organizations	Conduct high-quality analytical work Disseminate accurate and timely analyses of government performance to media, public, decisionmakers, other CSOs Convene experts and groups	Lack of resources Subject to funders' interests Limited or overly narrow technical expertise (including policy and institutional environment) Insufficient access to information
Community, activist, and faith-based organizations	Offer expertise and credibility in specific areas Disseminate information to members, the media, and the general public Organize advocacy efforts	Limited technical expertise Lack of objectivity (and therefore limited credibility) Insufficient access to information
Labor organizations	Disseminate information to members Organize pressure and advocacy efforts Undertake analytical work	Lack of objectivity Limited technical expertise Potential conflicts of interest with regard to public service provider groups
Business associations and private sector entities	Work for improved public services Exert pressure on decisionmakers	May only be attentive to matters of direct self-interest Limited technical expertise Lack of credibility with the general public

Bottom-up actors	Potential accountability functions	Potential obstacles
Academic institutions	Conduct high-quality analytical work	Work may be driven by funding sources' interests
	Disseminate findings to other experts and government actors	Work may be driven by availability of funds
		Analysis not accessible
		Analysis not timely
		Analysis not designed to influence government
Public commissions and oversight boards	Review government actions	Only used in limited contexts
	Provide a forum for discussing government performance	May lack resources and skill to conduct investigations

trading partners, strategic powers, and donors), supranational organizations (for example, the United Nations or the European Union), and multilateral organizations (for example, the International Monetary Fund and the World Bank), international NGOs (for example, Amnesty International, Greenpeace, environmental organizations, transparency and anticorruption organizations such as Transparency International), and multinational corporations. How these entities act as monitors of the government varies widely across countries. In general, however, countries are likely to be more receptive to these influences the more they desire, and would benefit from, participation in the global economy and multilateral organizations. A striking example is the efforts over recent years made by Eastern European countries to modify their legal framework and try to strengthen the capacities of public institutions in areas that are relevant to their potential membership in the European Union.[13]

Notes

1. See, for example, C. Nyman, F. Nilsson, and B. Rapp, "Accountability in Local Government: A Principal-Agent Perspective," *Journal of Human Resource Costing & Accounting* 9, no. 2 (2005): 123–37; J. Erik-Lane, *Public Administration and Public Management: The Principal-Agent Perspective* (New York: Routledge, 2005); R. Smith and M. Bertozzi, "Principals and Agents: An Explanatory Model for Public Budgeting," *Journal of Public Budgeting, Accounting, & Financial Management* 10, no. 3 (1998): 325–52.

2. Kathleen M. Eisenhardt, "Agency Theory: An Assessment and Review," *Academy of Management Review* 14, no. 1 (1989): 57–74.

3. ePolitix report, July 2, 2008. Beyond these members of the government, additional political appointees in the British system would include a relatively small number of political advisers to serve in ministries, and—over the longer term—replacement members of various public sector boards, corporations, and similar bodies.

4. Committee on Government Reform—Minority Staff, *The Growth of Political Appointees in the Bush Administration,* 109 Cong. 2 sess. (U.S. House of Representatives, May 2006). Note that the source used for this estimate does not include all appointees within the White House staff or the intelligence agencies and as such provides a lower bound.

5. See World Bank, *World Development Report 1997* (Oxford University Press), pp. 92–94.

6. R. N. Johnson and G. Libecap, *The Federal Civil Service System and the Problem of Bureaucracy: The Economics and Politics of Institutional Change* (University of Chicago Press, 1994), p. 154. See also Caroline Minter Hoxby, "How Teachers' Unions Affect Education Production," *Quarterly Journal of Economics* 111, no. 3 (1996): 671–718.

7. *Economist,* "Education in Mexico: Testing the Teachers," May 22, 2008.

8. Appendixes A to E present case studies of how decisions on budget allocations and implementation are handled in, respectively, Ghana, Kenya, Peru, Mexico, and Thailand.

9. Several variants of classification frameworks for different forms of accountability have been presented in the literature, including a differentiation between vertical and horizontal mechanisms and the long-route compared with the short-route model presented in the World Bank's *World Development Report 2004* (Oxford University Press).

10. During the British rule of India, the Indian Civil Service was composed of a small elite of (primarily British) officials occupying the most senior positions in the public administration. Upon independence, the ICS gave way to the similarly highly selective Indian Administrative Service, whose members continue to enjoy a high degree of security of tenure and to exercise enormous power. The competing demands and temptations facing IAS officers form a major theme of Edward Luce's study of the political economy of contemporary India, *In Spite of the Gods: The Strange Rise of Modern India* (New York: Anchor Books, 2007).

11. Our term *sideways accountability* is a modification of O'Donnell's *horizontal accountability.* See G. O'Donnell, "Horizontal Accountability in New Democracies," in *The Self-Restraining State: Power and Accountability in New Democracies,* edited by Andreas Schedler, Larry Diamond, and Marc F. Plattner (Boulder, Colo.: Lynne Rienner, 1999).

12. Mancur Olson, *The Logic of Collective Action: Public Goods and the Theory of Groups,* 2nd ed. (Harvard University Press, 1971).

13. There is, however, growing concern that at least some of the new members slackened or abandoned their efforts at governance reform once they were safely inside the EU and no longer faced the potential sanction of being denied admission. See, for example, *Economist,* "Corruption in Eastern Europe: Talking of Virtue, Counting the Spoons," May 24, 2008.

5

Interest Group Dynamics

The principal-agent model discussed in chapter 4 presents a number of important insights. At the same time, a model composed of citizens on one side and the government on another is an oversimplification of reality. As our discussion of the problem of collective action hinted, there may be multiple players in the game, each pushing for its own particular interests.

Various theories of political science seek to address this aspect of political systems by explaining how different interest groups compete to advance their interests through government action (or inaction). In classic pluralist theories, accountability is found in the overall design of the system, in the sense that, if there are many different groups competing, they will constantly challenge and negotiate with each other and no one group will dominate the system, to the extent that the various interests within society are represented in the system. The theories suggest that the ultimate outcome of such a competition will be government policies and practices that at least approximate some view of the common good.

By contrast, neopluralist and corporatist theories, while maintaining the focus on interest groups, emphasize the disproportionate power of certain groups: perhaps business interests in more developed countries or large landowners in some developing countries. Because these interest groups can exert such dominion over the system, it is argued, one cannot expect the resulting government policies and practice to come close to representing the common good.

In any case, it is clear that the real world setting within which government decisions take place (and the quality of governance is put to the test) does not involve a stately minuet among neutral, disinterested actors. Every participant has its own interests and an agenda to pursue, and the struggle for advantage among the participants can be fierce and ruthless.[1] Profit maximizers, government bodies, even nongovernmental bodies who proclaim their dedication to the larger good—no one is exempt from being a rent seeker in the unending contest to get a bigger share of whatever pie is up for grabs. Public sector entities, far from being above the fray, are often dogged fighters for their own turf, using their monopolistic powers in lawmaking, regulation setting, taxation, policing, justice, and so on to counter others' strengths.

Winners gain advantages at the expense of losers, and one of the frequent losers is apt to be the public good (however defined), which inherently has no active champion of its own. Some participants (governments, parliaments, courts) may *claim* to represent the public good, and some may defend it insofar as their own interests overlap with the public interest on some issues or for some period of time. But no one truly can always be counted on to suppress one's parochial interests.

Is Progress Possible?

An important feature of this relentless Darwinian battle is what Heller calls "the balloon problem."[2] Efforts to staunch behaviors inimical to the public good, even when successful in the arena where they are focused, are unlikely to be successful in a broader sense, since implacable rent seekers, who are clever at discovering new ways to game new systems, will find alternative routes to advance their interests. Push in on a balloon at one spot, and it will bulge out at another. For instance, anticorruption initiatives that close one set of loopholes will shift rent seekers' energies to finding ways to open others, which they will succeed in doing sooner or later. The net result, to the extent that the balloon problem cannot be contained by better designed and ever-vigilant public action, is that gains made on one front may be eroded at least partly by setbacks elsewhere.

Although the implications of interest group dynamics and the balloon problem can never be overcome entirely, some societies, at some times, clearly have been able to deal with these issues more effectively than others, achieving lower levels of corruption, abuse, and other behaviors contrary to the public interest. Understanding the better-performing cases—why they are different, what accounts for the choices that were made, what was done specifically and why it worked, and what can be learned from these countries for other countries in other situations—is obviously important in this context. If that evidence suggests ways to attain at least partial progress toward improved outcomes, then there is hope that the otherwise pessimistic conclusion that all effort is for naught (because the balloon is unforgiving) is not the only possible ending, to the degree that extraordinarily effective efforts can lead to at least partial improvement.

The simple answer, of course, is that the societies that have been able to limit corruption have typically possessed all, or nearly all, of the elements of an effective system of accountability—strong and independent law enforcement and courts, skilled investigative journalists and independent media outlets, professional civil servants, high-capacity and well-resourced monitoring organizations, and so on.

This implies that, over the longer term, the most crucial steps will involve working on the major policy enhancements and societal transformations that enable countries to shift from lower to higher standards of accepted behavior. These changes can be hard to bring about. Upgrading the essential elements of a country's investment climate—such as the rule of law, the enforcement of regulations, tax compliance, judicial probity, and macroeconomic responsibility—is clearly a desirable part of striving toward a fairer playing field for all, but real advances on those fronts require broad buy-in and support that is often difficult for some countries to put together. Likewise, significant "cleaning up" of prevailing practices in public services and other areas (for example, public procurement), so that there is less bribery and corruption, can have wide-ranging benefits, but that is rarely easy to effect. Even where countries have been able to implement and sustain substantial progress, many years have generally been required to achieve major results.

Just because the strongest systems are also the most complete and because system transformation is hard and time-consuming work does not mean that progress cannot be seen in developing countries before all the pieces are put in place. A few snapshots of success show how the fight for better governance (and against corruption) can lead to practical progress within a reasonable time frame.

Precedents Matter, Especially Legal Ones

Although those who benefit from corruption always seek new ways to continue to extract rents, successes are by no means fleeting. When a politician is caught stealing by investigative journalists and ends up in jail, a strong message is sent to other officials. When the courts are involved, successful precedents can establish new rules of the game in a way that helps all those pushing for stronger transparency, accountability, and good governance. For example, a Chilean civil society organization, the Terram Foundation, sought information on a controversial logging project and ended up taking its case to the Inter-American Court of Human Rights. That court ruled that, under the American Convention on Human Rights, the public had a general right of access to this kind of government information. This was an important victory for strengthening information access laws, which too often are poorly implemented and enforced in the region.[3]

Regional Efforts Can Help

In Central America, the transboundary nature of corruption has long been an obstacle to law enforcement, but the tables may now be turning. In the past, politicians in the region could transfer the funds they expropriated out of their country to another country in the region for safekeeping. This was possible because the national law enforcement agencies of the region did not communicate regularly or coordinate their anticorruption efforts. However, a recent initiative led by Panama with support from USAID brought the region's leading prosecutors together, and a system of cooperation was initiated to fight corruption. Because each agency is going after foreign politicians rather than its own entrenched officials, agencies may actually be better able to fight transboundary corruption even more effectively than they can against domestic corruption, once the infrastructure for cooperation is in place.[4]

Making Corruption More Difficult Matters

Few would assert that it is possible to eliminate corruption altogether. That is no reason not to try, because making it more difficult can make a big difference. The high profile report by the U.K. Commission for Africa, which looked closely at past efforts and potential strategies for fighting corruption, concluded that concrete steps could be taken, such as instituting mandatory transparent recording and reporting of natural resource revenues, to make it more difficult for government officials to steal public resources. While these steps might not prevent theft, the scale of corruption could be reduced substantially.[5]

Progress Requires Looking for Allies
(and Understanding Your Opponents)

A useful first step for understanding the functioning of interest groups in a given setting, and the potential scope for effective efforts to mobilize for better governance, is to try to map the interest group landscape in that setting. This involves trying to identify which groups are likely to be most influential on either side of major governance reform issues and why. An effective mapping of that landscape may not necessarily need to be done in lengthy, time-consuming detail, but it does need to be at least sufficiently thorough to indicate where some of the best entry points for action may be. Some of the key issues to consider in landscaping a country's interest groups are the following:

—*What are the primary private interest organizations in existence?*
   —What groups do they claim to support?
   —What kind of governance structure do they employ?
   —How well are they financed?
   —Is their technical competency sufficient for their mission in terms of analysis and advocacy?
   —Do they have access to the information they need to influence government?
   —What tactics do they use to influence government?
   —What benefits do they seek to obtain for their constituents?
—*What are the primary public interest organizations in existence?*
   —What aspects of the public good do they claim to support?
   —Are they member based, and if so, how many people do they represent?
   —What kind of governance structure do they employ?
   —How well are they financed?
   —Is their technical competency sufficient for their mission in terms of analysis and advocacy?
   —Do they have access to the information they need to influence government?
   —What tactics do they use to influence government?
   —What remedies do they suggest in terms of policy and institutional reform, budgeting, law enforcement, for example?
   —Do they frequently partner with any other organizations?
—*What groups of citizens may be underrepresented within interest groups?*
   —Do they have existing social institutions that could function as government monitors or interest organizations?
   —Do they have sufficient economic resources to support an interest organization?
   —Could they obtain funding from domestic or external sources?
   —Are there methods of overcoming problems in organizing themselves that are caused by the fact that they are geographically dispersed?

By asking these questions at the country-specific level, would-be governance reformers (and their potential allies inside or outside the country) can
begin to gain a more realistic sense of how it might be possible to mount
efforts to overcome the collective action problem.

A carefully conducted mapping exercise can help to identify potential allies
and likely staunch opponents one issue at a time. The nineteenth-century
statesman Lord Palmerston famously observed that "nations have no permanent friends or allies, they only have permanent interests," and this dictum can
also be applied to domestic interest groups. Governance reformers may find
that a group that opposes them on one particular issue may prove to be a
potential ally on a different front.

In this way, mapping may also help governance reformers identify which
issues it makes sense to push on first: to find the low-hanging fruit and zero
in on potentially popular reforms facing limited opposition, which could help
establish precedents in areas that initially look harder to attack head on.

Notes

1. The seminal work on the topics covered in this chapter was done by Thomas
Heller at Stanford University.

2. Heller uses the "balloon problem" metaphor to illustrate the importance of carefully planning anticorruption interventions so as to anticipate and address or avoid
undesired outcomes.

3. Martha Farmelo, "Stop the Press: Censorship on the Rise in Latin American
Democracies," International Relations Center, April 20, 2007 (www.worldpress.org/
Americas/2761.cfm).

4. USAID, "Success Story: Prosecutors Team Up to Fight Corruption," May 2, 2006
(www.usaid.gov/stories/panama/ss_pa_corruption.html).

5. Commission for Africa, *Our Common Interest: Report of the Commission for
Africa* (March 11, 2005), pp. 133–56.

6 | Signals and Actions

Thus far, we have looked only in the broadest of terms at the ways in which the different actors we have been discussing—citizens, the public sector, and other sectors such as business—interact and communicate with each other. But the specific ways in which actors communicate their goals and intentions can make a great difference to outcomes. And this is particularly relevant to the design and effectiveness of any concrete efforts by citizens and intermediaries to try to improve standards of governance.

This chapter explains the significance of these aspects by drawing on insights from signal theory. *Signals* and *actions* are terms used to describe the methods different individuals and groups use to express demands—or respond to them.

Why Signals and Actions Matter

Consider, first, some of the ways in which citizens send signals to their government. They may act through voting, responses to opinion pollsters, participation in the media, public debate, boycotts, street demonstrations, armed resistance, or many other means. Familiar examples include the strong messages that voters sometimes send in elections, as they have in Kenya in recent decades; the seesaw shifting of public opinion that changes the fortunes of leaders, as in Italy periodically; the mounting opposition, domestically and internationally, that toppled apartheid in South Africa; the success of Gandhi in using public opinion in Great Britain and India to gain independence; the pot-banging demonstrations that have become a popular form of protest against unpopular governments in countries like Chile and Argentina; and the armed conflict that spilt Eritrea and Ethiopia.

Citizens' actions sometimes arise as a response to earlier actions taken by the public sector. Indonesia's citizens took to the streets in the late 1990s in protest against government corruption and poor economic performance. In other cases, citizens' actions reflect a more generalized reaction to events, as when Africans, driven by fundamental economic forces, go to Europe seeking work.

The public sector in turn transmits signals and actions to citizens. Examples of government signals and actions include legislative, executive, and judicial decisions that affect citizens' pocketbooks, liberties, and opportunities; the use of the bully pulpit and propaganda to influence popular thinking; enforcement actions that include fines, incarceration, and intimidation; special privileges such as trade preferences or tax loopholes; and the granting and withholding of citizenship.

Other sectors also exchange signals and actions with citizens and the public sector to affect the outcomes of interactions. Corporations, for example, send signals and take actions with respect to government (through lobbying) and citizens (through advertising their products).

Some signals and actions go directly from the sender to their intended recipient. Other signals and actions go through intermediaries. Citizens, in particular, may rely on intermediaries such as the media, civil society organizations, lobbyists, shareholder groups, and a vast array of other entities. (See figure 6-1.)

The effectiveness of signals and actions—including an understanding of factors that either amplify or constrain their effectiveness in achieving their intended effect—represent a crucial part of this book's overall story of how citizens and intermediaries can try to improve standards of governance.

What Determines Whether Signals and Actions Hit the Goal?

Signal theory contributes the insight that there are several steps involved in delivering a signal, from the point it is first conceived until the point it is finally acted upon. A stylized breakdown of these stages would include formulation, transmission, reception, response, and feedback and backlash. At each stage, there are skills and resources (financial, information, and so on) that may be needed for the effective implementation of the signaling process. Problems that arise anywhere along this chain can affect the final result.

Figure 6-1. *Signals and Actions*

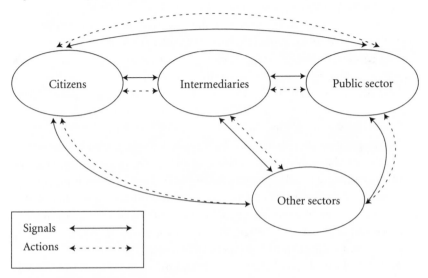

In the formulation stage, a huge amount of thought, organization, and motivation is often required, especially when signals that challenge the status quo need to break through strong resistance. The strategy of the civil rights movement in the United States in the third quarter of the twentieth century did not come together overnight or without extensive reflection, negotiation, and outreach.

At the transmission stage, there are many occasions when vital signals do not actually get sent, or when they are not sent sufficiently vigorously and relentlessly to overcome barriers or noise. Minority groups or marginalized peoples may be especially constrained by obstacles that make it difficult for them to speak out or even to vote. In multilevel government structures, such as in China, India, and other federal systems, signal loss may be high if messages need to wend their way upward from village to county to province to the national government.

At the reception stage, there can be crucial logistical and organizational questions, as well as behavioral and attitudinal issues. Do government agencies deal effectively with public comments on proposed regulations? Do leaders ensure that bureaucrats take citizens' signals seriously?

At the response stage, signals often fall on deaf ears, as when authoritarian regimes ignore citizen concerns or nonresponsive bureaucracies disregard or fail to follow up on public input. Unintended consequences, wrong policy choices, or poor administration take a heavy toll too. When business leaders in some developing countries in the second half of the twentieth century convinced their governments to adopt currency exchange rates at odds with what market conditions would support, they did not realize that resulting black market exchange rates and economic distortions would result in more harm to them than the good they sought. Parisians in 1789 took actions—mobbing the streets—that unleashed changes that few had expected or initially sought.[1]

Further, when an action reaches those it affects, the nature of its impact depends on how they receive it—the feedback and backlash stage. When China's post-Mao leaders set about revamping economic policy, farmers, employees, investors, and entrepreneurs responded robustly, resulting in three decades of extraordinary growth. By contrast, attempts in recent years by several west European governments to liberalize the regulation of labor markets have been either blocked by large-scale street protests, as in France, or eroded by subsequent policy concessions, as in Germany.

Table 6-1 illustrates the different steps and the skills and resources generally required to execute them for the specific example of signals and actions sent from the public to the government (obviously governments follow similar processes in sending signals and taking actions to affect the beliefs or actions of the public).

Functional Outcomes

The ultimate goal of many actors within civil society is to change the way that government functions. This section reviews some of the functional outcomes that signals and actions from civil society might be directed at achieving.

Replace the Agent

The most obvious way a government entity can be replaced is through elections. However, as already discussed in chapter 4, elections may have multiple limitations. Beyond this, the specific target of citizens' concerns or of a monitoring effort may not have been elected (either individually or collectively), which means that replacement of the agent would have to happen through administrative action. In more extreme cases, the replacement of a high-level elected agent may occur also through nonelectoral means: for example, the impeachment of a president for misconduct or the ouster of an administration by popular direct action (such as the mass public demonstra-

Table 6-1. *Steps in the Signals and Actions Process (Public to Government)*

Signal or action step	Skills and resources required for effectiveness
1. *Formulation.* The substance of the senders' concerns is developed and refined. This can involve accessing and analyzing information on government actions and potential remedies. The senders must also determine the details of how they will convey their concerns, including what transmission mechanisms and strategies they will employ.	Technical capacity to analyze government activities, including raw data and complex regulatory, legal, and policy materials Communications outreach skills for formulating effective messages, particularly when the public is targeted Understanding of the available signaling pathways and potential partners and accountability mechanisms (for example, courts, parliaments, law enforcement) that can be leveraged
2. *Transmission.* The signal passes from the senders to the targeted recipients through channels that may accurately convey the message or weaken or distort it. The strength of the message may be enhanced through its replication by other senders (if, for example, other interest groups re-transmit the signal or members of the general public express support for the signal). Characteristics of the transmission channels used (such as radio, television, newsprint, or person-to-person) or impedance factors (such as poor choice of medium for the target audience) can be critical to the effectiveness of transmission.	Access to transmission instruments, which itself depends on, among other things, the openness of the instrument to messages critical of government, the financial resources of the sender, and the credibility of the sender Existing partnerships that can be leveraged to enhance transmission (for example, NGOs with lobbying capabilities and social institutions that can disseminate the message to other potential senders)
3. *Reception (the endpoint of the transmission).* The signal reaches the targeted government entity and is "read" by government officials. The targeted entity may also be a governmental accountability mechanism (such as an ombudsman, an auditor, law enforcement) that has the capacity to apply pressure to or enjoin action by another government entity.	Efficient transmission of the signal within government from receiver to decision-maker (that is, lack of "noise" in the internal transmission) Understanding of the signal accurately by government actors Governmental accountability mechanisms that are reasonably independent, adequately resourced, and open to signals and actions critical of government

Table 6-1 *(continued)*

Signal or action step	Skills and resources required for effectiveness
	Credible and sufficiently frequent public opinion polling that is available for the government to test the strength of signals and for senders to reference as evidence of signal strength
4. *Response.* The actions taken by the recipient in response to the signal.	Sufficient accountability pressures associated with the signal such that government decisionmakers can justify meaningful action
	Government will and the capacity to respond effectively (for example, it must have sufficient control over the bureaucracy and the technical, legal, and financial capacity to address identified problems)
	Monitoring by sender and its partners (that is, other independent monitoring organizations, independent media, external entities) of actions that the government takes in response (including ensuring that government does more than pay lip service to the signal)
5. *Feedback and backlash.* These are actions taken by the original sender and other civil society entities as a reaction to the government's response to the original signal. This is an important step since, as interest group theory suggests, a governmental action will often be seen as positive by some interest groups and negative by others.	Sufficient resources and institutional stability for the sender to remain engaged Other independent monitoring organizations with sufficient capacity to monitor and analyze to determine whether and how government actions adversely affect their interests

tions that led to the successive resignations of former Bolivian presidents Gonzalo Sánchez de Lozada and Carlos Mesa during the course of 2003).

Compel Behavioral Change by Pressure or Other Means

Citizens or civil society intermediaries can also seek to compel a change in the government entity's behavior by bringing pressure to bear on the government entity directly or by leveraging available enforcement mechanisms (for example, courts or the parliament).

Adjust the Policy and Institutional Environment

The behavior of government entities can also be changed by adjusting the policy and institutional environment within which they operate. This can be done by changing the incentives within the system to align the interests of the agent more closely with those of the principal or by changing the system of controls and sanctions (negative incentives). Efforts may also be made to reallocate resources away from low-priority programs (or poorly performing government entities) toward more promising uses.

Adjust Monitoring Efforts

A possible response to the results of efforts by the civil society to monitor governments may be that civil society groups find that they need to adjust the nature of their monitoring itself. Intensified monitoring may be indicated, or efforts retargeted to other government actors, or further information may need to be sought.

Engage in Dialogue

A response might well be to engage the government entity in discussions, bargaining, negotiations, or any form of give-and-take that could result in mutual education and eventual changes in attitude or action.

Note

1. For the argument that political change during the French Revolution repeatedly went beyond the initial demands of almost all participants, see, for example, Sylvia Neely, *A Concise History of the French Revolution* (Lanham, Md.: Rowman and Littlefield, 2008).

7

Political Systems

So far, our discussion of interactions between citizens (and civil society intermediaries) and governments has largely abstracted from the specifics of different national political systems. Yet it is obvious that the potential ability of citizens and NGOs to influence their government will be very different depending on whether they are working within a well-established electoral democracy, in which there are competitive elections, a lively media, and respect for the rule of law and freedom of speech, or a single party autocracy, in which the regime controls all media and criticism of the ruling elite invites prosecution or regime-sanctioned violence. Similarly, the mechanisms and tactics that aspiring reformers might use, and the immediate goals they might realistically pursue, will differ enormously between the two situations.

The discussion becomes more interesting once it is recognized that a large proportion of real-world political systems, especially in developing or transition countries, do not correspond neatly to one or the other of these two polar cases. Most countries are neither a perfect liberal democracy nor a complete and total autocracy but fit somewhere in between—they are political hybrids.

Political scientists have adopted at least two different analytical approaches to try to impose intellectual order on the world of political hybrids. One approach is to try to create typologies of political systems as a whole: standardized types of regimes with which actual systems could be compared. An alternative approach is to identify certain key attributes of regimes and try to categorize these attributes along multidimensional scales.

Typologies of Political Systems

Political scientists have often begun their classification schemes with the distinction that was made above between democracy and authoritarianism and have then sought to capture the existence of various hybrid models.

—Samuel Huntington proposed a theoretical framework (including references to *praetorian* versus *civic* systems) that allowed for the possibility of such hybrids as popularly elected authoritarian governments and rigidly elitist democracies.[1]

—Guillermo O'Donnell, Philippe Schmitter, and Laurence Whitehead proposed a classification of hybrid systems that introduced the terms *dictablanda* (liberal authoritarianism) and *democradura* (illiberal democracy).[2] Other scholars coined terms like *pseudo-democracies* and *electoral authoritarianism.*

—Steven Levitsky and Lucan Way introduced the term *competitive authoritarianism* to describe systems in which a government that is authoritarian nonetheless allows elections and reasonable competition from opposition parties.[3]

—Marina Ottaway used the term *semi-authoritarianism* to describe cases in which dictators allow a measure of democratization to sustain their regimes in the face of international and domestic pressure for liberalization.[4]

—Larry Diamond produced a comprehensive review of this literature and attempted to synthesize its insights into a sixfold typology of political systems: liberal democracy, electoral democracy, competitive authoritarianism, hegemonic electoral authoritarianism, closed authoritarianism, and ambiguous.[5]

Diamond's categories reflect the governance processes of the country and the strength of the rule of law and civil liberty protection. This two-way classification helps make his approach particularly useful in the present context. His six categories can be compressed into four:

—*Liberal democracy*: Free, competitive elections; political pluralism; strong rule of law; and broad-based protection of civil rights

—*Electoral democracy*: Free elections, though not necessarily entirely competitive; some pluralism but power concentrated; rule of law and civil rights weakly or discriminately protected

—*Electoral authoritarianism*: Somewhat free elections, but limited competition, or outcomes not respected; little pluralism or rule of law; and civil rights poorly protected

—*Closed authoritarianism*: No pretense at democracy; almost by definition, ordinary citizens have very limited opportunities to hold the government accountable outside of the (highly difficult) development of a sufficiently broad-based social movement or via a coup

A further category, *failing or conflict-ridden states*, might be added. These types of states include countries where war, deep ethnic divisions, or other sources of strife have rendered the government dysfunctional. Here, citizens cannot expect to effect improvements in governance because the government does not have the capacity to receive and respond to their signals.

Digging Deeper

The findings from this literature offer a useful reminder to potential campaigners for good governance that country political systems cover a wide gamut and that specific country realities will be key determinants of the realistic strategies that campaigners can employ. That said, there are further dimensions that are worth adding to the models discussed so far.

First, political systems may change over time, either gradually or abruptly.

—In Mexico during the latter years of the seventy-one-year reign of the Institutional Revolutionary Party, for example, aspects of the emerging competitive democracy overlapped with surviving elements of autocracy.

—The multiple election victories of Hugo Chávez in Venezuela ushered in a change from a two-party system, however flawed and formulaic, to a new model of populist authoritarianism.

—The collapse of Soviet domination of the satellite countries in Eastern Europe sparked rapid changes in political systems. In many cases, a rapid transition from the previous communist system to new models that more-or-less closely approximated liberal democracy was negotiated between elements of the old regime and those who until that point had been considered outsiders, such as the labor leader Lech Walesa in Poland or the dissident playwright Vaclav Havel in Czechoslovakia. However, variations at the national level were substantial, including the extent to which former insiders were able to perpetuate some hold on power.

Second, the standard literature's taxonomies place countries mostly on a single spectrum ranging from liberal democracy at one extreme to closed authoritarianism on the other. This one-dimensionality, however, conceals important distinctions between different countries. In a more nuanced model, three scales are used to capture key elements in different political systems (figure 7-1):

—*Executive power*: the degree to which power is concentrated in a few hands, especially those of the head of state

Figure 7-1. *Key Elements of Different Political Systems*

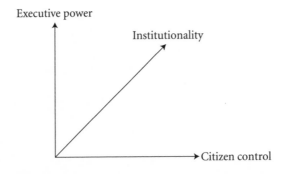

—*Citizen control*: the degree to which citizens' voice in public discourse and votes at the ballot box are taken seriously and influence outcomes

—*The strength of institutions*: sometimes referred to as *institutionality*, indicating the degree to which duly adopted laws, rights, and practices are respected

While there are often significant correlations among these three dimensions, there are also abundant cases where essential information would be lost by compressing the three scales into one. As the country examples in table 7-1 show, exceptions to the usually expected combinations of high and

Table 7-1. *Executive Power, Institutionality, and Citizen Control: Country Examples*

	Executive power			
	High		Low	
	Institutionality		Institutionality	
Citizen control	High	Low	High	Low
High	India, Israel, Botswana (2007)	Venezuela during Hugo Chávez's first two years	Bolivia, when Morales was elected (2005)	Indonesia, when protests toppled the government (1998)
Low	China, Singapore, Malawi (2007)	Zimbabwe (2007)	Argentina under Duhalde (2002)	Somalia, when chaos gripped the country (1992)

Table 7-2. *Executive Power, Institutionality, and Citizen Control: South Africa at Different Times*

	Executive power			
	High		Low	
	Institutionality		Institutionality	
Citizen control	High	Low	High	Low
High	The Mandela government, at its apex	Initial years of the Mandela government, as the rules for the post-apartheid era were being crafted	Phase III of the transition period from apartheid to Mandela	Phase I of the transition period from apartheid to Mandela
Low	The apartheid government, at its apex	The apartheid government as it eroded under pressure	Phase II of the transition period from apartheid to Mandela	Just before apartheid ended

low scores are not uncommon. Table 7-2 illustrates that these indicators can be equally useful in identifying changes in governance structures within a country across time.

Summing up, efforts by citizen-based groups to influence standards of governance at the level of the country need to be informed by a realistic understanding of the realities of the specific political system. These realities can determine the extent of the space within which civil society is able to function and may set limits to feasible tactics to be used, at least in the short term. At the same time, systems can change, whether by evolution, as in the case of Mexico and many East Asian countries, or by more abrupt change, such as that experienced by much of Eastern Europe. Active efforts on the part of civil society can be among the most important contributors to change for the better in either case.

Notes

1. Samuel Huntington, *Political Order in Changing Societies* (Yale University Press, 1968), pp. 79–82.

2. Guillermo O'Donnell, Philippe C. Schmitter, and Laurence Whitehead, *Transitions from Authoritarian Rule: Tentative Conclusions about Uncertain Democracies* (Johns Hopkins University Press, 1986), p. 9.

3. Steven Levitsky and Lucan Way, "The Rise of Competitive Authoritarianism," *Journal of Democracy* 13, no. 2 (April 2002): 51–65.

4. Marina Ottaway, *Democracy Challenged: The Rise of Semi-Authoritarianism* (Washington: Carnegie Endowment for International Peace, 2003).

5. Larry Diamond, "Elections without Democracy: Thinking of Hybrid Regimes," *Journal of Democracy* 13, no. 2 (April 2002): 21–35.

8 | Interventions

Previous chapters have provided the basis for a better understanding of the actors and mechanisms involved in existing systems of accountability. The present chapter focuses on types of actions (*interventions*) for trying to improve governance that may be open to domestic groups like CSOs and that may deserve support from international groups such as NGOs, foundations, and multilateral development agencies.

Working through Existing Channels to Promote Change

Application of the analytical framework discussed in previous chapters should make it possible to create a map of the actors, institutions, and processes involved in the functioning of a given country's system of governance and accountability. This is important because research shows that a primary obstacle for CSOs trying to influence government policies and practices is inadequate understanding of the policy and institutional context within which they operate.[1]

A possible framework for pulling together key information and ideas about the overall functioning of a country's existing system of accountability and society's priorities is the matrix proposed by Paul Collier (table 8-1).

The matrix makes it possible to summarize evaluations of the strength of the different channels of accountability in the country, with particular reference to the potential priority areas for improvement, which might be in the direction of greater effectiveness, efficiency, equity, honesty, and so on. The matrix could be one of the tools employed in undertaking a country mapping exercise.

Table 8-1. *Paul Collier Matrix*

	Top down		Bottom up		Sideways		External	
	Ex ante	Ex post	Ex ante	Ex post	Ex ante	Ex post	Ex ante	Ex post
Effective?								
Efficient?								
Equitable?								
Pro-poor?								
Honest?								
Sustainable?								
Impact on problem of special interests?								

For organizations seeking to operate effectively within the existing rules of the game, a map can be used to identify viable strategies for achieving results. Users can work through various existing channels and processes to promote change, assessing at each step whether the necessary ingredients for success are in place, and if not, what alternatives may be available. Users can identify additional mechanisms that they can leverage (for example, pressure from international donors or information access laws) to enhance their effectiveness.

Using the existing system effectively may also contribute to changes in the system itself. First, successful accountability actions (efforts to monitor the government that succeed in improving performance) set important precedents that often can be replicated more broadly in the same country. Second, successful actions can have a deterrent effect by demonstrating to government officials that abuse can be discovered and sanctioned. Third, by drawing wider public attention to poor government performance, accountability actions may have a catalytic impact in sparking more extensive reform campaigns. Accordingly, one lesson for CSOs is that they need to make the most out of their successes.

Identifying Weak Points for Strengthening

Beyond operating effectively within the existing rules of the game, some organizations may seek to change those rules for the better. Here, too, having undertaken a mapping exercise will help identify, prioritize, and coordinate potential interventions. In the tables that follow, we revisit some of the key elements in overall accountability systems discussed in earlier chapters (interest

Box 8-1. *Whose Goals? Whose Priorities?*

This book operates from the standpoint that more accountability and transparency are better than less, and less corruption better than more. These preferences seem to be widely shared. Public opinion polls around the world, including surveys targeting the poor, reveal a high degree of shared resentment of officials who feather their own nests at the expense of the general population. Not long ago, it was common to hear arguments that "a little corruption" helped grease the wheels in developing countries or that it was an intrinsic part of local values in such and such a region. But as evidence has mounted of the negative links between corruption and development and of the injustices imposed on ordinary people by unaccountable bureaucrats, policemen, or judges, these arguments are being met with more skepticism.

That said, valid questions can be asked about how far people in different societies necessarily share identical goals and priorities for improving the functioning of their governments. In many transition and developing countries in particular, while all may agree that there is substantial work to be done to improve accountability and governance, different citizens, intermediaries, and political groupings may attach different levels of importance to improving, say, the efficiency or the honesty of the administration. People may have significantly different views over the relative importance of improving the quality of services to the broad mass of the population, who perhaps are urban dwellers or the members of the majority ethnic group in the country, as opposed to special efforts to help the poorer groups catch up, such as those living in more remote rural areas or the members of historically marginalized ethic groups or castes. Even where people agree over broad goals for the society, they may make different judgments over what improvements are likely to be most politically feasible in the immediate future.

groups, governmental controls, and signal and action processes). The purpose is to examine typical problems that can arise in each of these areas and then to indicate potential interventions that might be relevant in each case. These lists are illustrative rather than comprehensive. Equally, the applicability of a particular intervention is something that would need to be reviewed with care in the context of any specific country situation.

Government Controls

Efforts to improve the functioning of accountability forces frequently focus, at least initially, on governmental controls and accountability mechanisms

Additionally, as already seen, countries do not divide simply between unimpeachable democracies and indefensible dictatorships. There are hybrids, and not even all fully functioning democracies are identical twins in the ways they address some of the key challenges of accountability and transparency discussed in this study. Distinctions do sometimes have to be made. Some countries that may not measure up to the highest standards of open, competitive democracy nonetheless offer considerable scope for country-level work by outside groups to help improve the welfare of the ordinary people. Others, though, represent the extreme cases, where a dictator oppresses the general public and seems only concerned with his own well-being and survival.

Where does this leave outside players—multilateral agencies or NGOs—who seek to help improve governance standards around the world? Nothing written here should bring that broad goal into question. But a degree of humility may sometimes be in order, including recognizing the need to take into account individual country realities along with a willingness to listen to the perceptions of credible domestic actors on local conditions and priorities, rather than wading into each country with the same cookie-cutter approach. Large agencies such as the World Bank have developed elaborate systems of consultation with domestic civil society on a country's overall development priorities, for example, in the context of Poverty Reduction Strategy Papers. Consultations on this scale will be beyond the resources of most NGOs, but the broader principle of listening first could usefully be adopted by all international governance players working at the national level, whether large or small. In the most extreme country cases, agencies may have to be willing to wait for changed political conditions to make it possible for meaningful work to be done on governance within the country concerned.

(see table 8-2). This focus is understandable, and there is already significant expertise among the various organizations involved in these areas that can be drawn on to plan and implement effective interventions. What is needed is more of these efforts and greater coordination of interventions to increase the likelihood that sought-after reforms will be implemented and maintained.

Interest Groups

When the role of interest groups in a given system is considered, it may be common to find that some well-established groups—such as big businesses or farming interests—are far more effective at expressing their interests and

Table 8-2. *Government Controls: Typical Problems and Potential Interventions*

Typical problems	Potential interventions
Top political leadership may seek to gain greater control over governmental entities that provide control mechanisms and thereby reduce accountability.	Maintain professional and politically independent accountability entities that are responsible for control functions, such as auditors, inspectors general, law enforcement: —Encourage IFIs to promote institutional reforms supporting political independence of such entities —Support exchange programs for individuals carrying out these functions to learn how they operate effectively in other countries —Publish reports on the performance of these entities —Train local media to report on good or bad performance
Internal accountability mechanisms lack independence, financial and technical capacity, or legal power to fulfill their functions effectively.	Work with multilateral and bilateral organizations to promote the strengthening of key entities Encourage donors to tie aid to performance in these areas Encourage domestic monitoring organizations and independent media to document and publicize shortcomings of these mechanisms
Personal, familial, or social or political relationships between politicians and control mechanism personnel can reduce the effectiveness of internal accountability mechanisms.	Precisely define the obligations and limit the discretion of these entities Limit political control over officials following appointment Require certain positions to be filled through standard career hiring and promotional practices (that is, no political appointees)
The state has the tendency to roll back or fail to adequately comply with information access, disclosure, and consultation obligations.	Conduct ongoing benchmarking of state performance in these areas Encourage opposition political parties to commit to support for these mechanisms Train journalists to report on shortcomings in these areas Encourage donors to tie aid to performance in these areas
The state may only disclose large volumes of raw information on performance that average citizens do not have time or the capacity to analyze.	Support the efforts of organizations that can engage in high-quality and credible monitoring of government performance Promote policies facilitating effective disclosure (that is, timely and accessible information release, plain language writing, well-organized and summarized materials)

Table 8-3. *Interest Groups: Typical Problems and Interventions*

Typical problems	Potential interventions
Members of the general public face government-imposed obstacles to the formation and operation of public interest organizations critical of government.	Leverage international pressure on government: —Initiate coordinated efforts to promote reform through donor organizations, multinational corporations, international NGOs, and other external actors —Promote the application of international legal regimes such as the UN Convention against Corruption (specifically Article 13, Participation of society) Support the work of international independent monitoring organizations that have the freedom to monitor and criticize governments
Citizens face collective action problems in organizing to promote their interests (especially poor groups that may lack financial resources, are geographically dispersed, and have limited awareness and understanding of government activities).	Work to create an enabling environment for the formation of NGOs and, more generally, of membership-based organizations within civil society: —Establish rules for preferential tax treatment for public interest organizations —Simplify incorporation procedures —Provide guidance on forming and operating public interest organizations in different contexts Strengthen existing organizations (for example, academic entities, tribal structures, faith-based organizations, labor unions) that have the potential to expand their functions to serve as government monitors Explore the application of pro-poor organization models that have been proven effective elsewhere Support citizen education, including efforts to "translate" key messages into everyday language that resonates with the general public
Even if citizens have resources, they lack incentives to organize or support public interest organizations because of the lack of confidence in achieving an impact.	Establish and support ways, domestically and internationally, to highlight public interest organizations' work and impacts: —Host forums for organizations to discuss their efforts and achievements —Train local news media to report on the work of public interest organizations —Produce high-profile reports and publications covering their efforts Recognize the work of effective public interest organizations through award programs Provide clear pathways for public interest organizations to provide input through external actors (for example, IFIs, bilateral donors, international NGOs)

(continued)

Table 8-3 *(continued)*

Typical problems	Potential interventions
Citizen movements and public interest groups lack understanding of the policy and institutional environment and therefore pursue ineffective strategies.	Provide technical guidance and training to these organizations based on up-to-date assessments of the current environment

Special interest groups with the potential to capture private benefits tend to exert excessive influence, with some tending to develop "iron triangle" relationships with their regulators (this is sometimes referred to as *regulatory capture,* a situation in which the regulator identifies primarily with the interests of the groups the regulator is supposed to regulate), compared with the influence that public interest groups can generate.	Require disclosure of special interest financing and lobbying activities
	
	Require disclosure of all budgeting as well as bidding and contracting decisions
	
	Support engagement of public interest, independent monitoring organizations in sectors susceptible to abuse:
	    —Provide project funding to independent monitoring organizations interested in studying government behavior in high-risk sectors (for example, energy, agriculture, transport, defense)
	    —Provide technical assistance to organizations working in these sectors
	
	Leverage support from international actors involved in the problem area, such as multinational corporations involved in the sector

The public tends to support public interest groups focusing on issues of interest to the middle class, such as environmental quality or international human rights, and gives less support to groups working on issues of interest to the poor, such as homelessness or food aid.	Encourage existing public interest groups to include pro-poor initiatives in their agendas:
	    —Provide project funding for pro-poor work
	    —Recognize pro-poor work through high-profile publications, discussions in international forums, or awards programs
	    —Provide technical assistance to organizations working in sectors that are most relevant to the concerns of the poor
	
	Require public agencies to report on the impact of public services on the poor
	
	Train journalists to report on poverty-related issues

Special interest groups quickly find new and sometimes more covert means of continuing to exert undue influence on government after more obvious pathways are closed (the "balloon problem").	Work with monitoring organizations to identify underlying interests Provide ongoing financial support to organizations engaged in government monitoring and give them flexibility to adjust their monitoring efforts to new areas

Table 8-4. *Signals and Actions: Typical Problems and Interventions*

Typical problems	*Potential interventions*
Public interest organizations have a low capacity to assess government performance so as to produce strong evidence of shortcomings and articulate persuasive messages.	Support strengthening of domestic capacity to identify and implement solutions (for example, by building the capacity of local think tanks that can provide high-quality input to legislators and bureaucrats)
General public may rely on centralized media instruments, such as television and radio, that are more susceptible to control by powerful interests and the state.	Encourage the development of alternative ways to transmit information, for example, online news media, independent news radio, and dissemination of information through social networks
News media, even if not controlled by the state, tend to lack credibility, or they do not reach many citizens, especially the poor.	Enhance the capacity of promising independent media instruments: for example, train journalists and provide financial and technical assistance to high-quality news media
	Utilize information technology tools to disseminate high-quality information to dispersed populations
Signals from the public can be distorted while being transmitted to pertinent decisionmakers after initial receipt by the government (particularly when signals are received locally and decisions are made centrally).	Encourage decentralization of authority to lower levels
	Encourage governments to adopt more rigorous mechanisms for receiving and tracking citizen input
Decisionmakers pay lip service to public interests and act in accordance with special interests.	Publish ratings of legislators' records
	Enable citizen lawsuits to enforce government obligations
	Require bureaucrats to document their responses to public input
	Support groups that have the technical capacity and credibility that is needed to shed light on the state's failures or inability to deliver on promises

(continued)

Table 8-4 *(continued)*

Typical problems	Potential interventions
Lack of political competition undermines institutional culture (with no accountability, there is less demand for improved performance), and leaders do not address problems even when these have been clearly identified.	Build the demand and appreciation for evidence-based information, by supporting opinion polling work, for example
	Spotlight the extent to which evidence-based information is or is not used, by publishing ratings or op-ed pieces on this issue
	Leverage external pressure and peer pressure through benchmarking and other strategies to spotlight shortcomings and incentivize a response
Instead of addressing citizens' concerns, governments use co-option and divide-and-conquer tactics.	Monitor and report on state-led efforts to use such tactics
	Support independent media and other information dissemination mechanisms that are capable of escaping government co-option and expressing viewpoints independent of government

objectives than other groups in the society, which might include ordinary consumers and users of public services or members of minority ethnic or religious communities.

How should those who aspire to improve governance approach these types of disparities? First, if one recognizes that effective pluralist systems work by allowing all legitimate voices to be heard, it will usually be a more realistic goal to try to strengthen the voice of those who have traditionally been voiceless— and to attack any artificial barriers to such representation—than to mount a frontal assault on the ability of better-established groups to represent their own interests. Second, a healthy system will typically include at least some public interest organizations that make good faith efforts to represent the general welfare and perform objective monitoring, analysis, and advocacy functions. This in turn will help provide countervailing power to the influence of narrow special interests upon government.

Table 8-3 presents some of the typical problems that arise in this area and potential interventions available to public interest groups seeking to make their government more accountable.

Signals and Actions

The signals and actions processes in a country obviously overlap with the functioning of interest groups and governmental controls, and all of the problems and interventions listed in tables 8-2 and 8-3 could also be included here in table 8-4. In the context of identifying interventions, however, focusing on the signals and actions processes also highlights additional elements of the chain of accountability that have not arisen in the above analyses.

Deciding which interventions are appropriate in any given country setting at any given time will be a key output of application of the analytical framework at the country level. This forms the subject of chapter 9.

Note

1. See Julius Court and others, "Policy Engagement: How Civil Society Can Be More Effective" (London: Overseas Development Institute, 2006), p. 17.

PART
III

*Operationalizing
the Framework*

9

Application at Country Level

Earlier chapters have presented a series of models relevant to the book's central concern with the quality of governance, including levels of accountability and transparency and the control of corruption. The discussion has placed special emphasis on the potential for civil society groups to play a stronger role in promoting higher standards of governance, while also warning of some of the obstacles to be expected, including resistance from interests that benefit from opaque public decisionmaking.

Many of the models and insights offered in the earlier parts of the book are derived from theoretical work in various branches of the social sciences. However, the book itself is not intended primarily as a contribution to theory. It is designed, first and foremost, to have operational relevance by offering practical intellectual tools for groups interested in improving governance. These may include domestic CSOs as well as their potential allies, such as would-be reformers within government or in domestic politics, the media, and possible external partners including international foundations, bilateral donors, and multilateral development agencies.

One of the specific roles the book is intended to play is to provide a reference for groups interested in assessing key governance issues at the individual country level. This chapter discusses some of the questions likely to arise in carrying out such an assessment.

Applying the Framework—A Toolkit, Not a Blueprint

The framework provided in this book potentially could help guide a country-level assessment regardless of who is actually undertaking the assessment.

The assessment could be undertaken by (or on behalf of) a multilateral agency, a bilateral donor, an international foundation, or a government agency within the country, or a locally based NGO. In any of these cases, the framework should help raise relevant issues.

However, application of the same broad framework does not mean that each of these types of players would necessarily make an identical assessment of the same country. Each group has its own areas of interest. A donor agency may want to know more about the overall environment in which its resources are being spent. A foundation may be looking for specific opportunities to strengthen domestic civil society. A local NGO may be looking for ways in which it could itself play a stronger role in strengthening governance in the country, and so on. So, in planning a country assessment, each may be looking to generate the answers to a different set of questions.

In this context, some foundations by their nature may place their emphasis largely or exclusively on the potential to enhance the role of civil society. Other agencies, by contrast, may be agnostic on the means by which governance might be improved and equally prepared to focus, for example, on strengthening watchdogs within the public sector, such as auditors, ombudsmen, parliamentary committees, or the judicial system. This chapter seeks to provide sufficiently broad coverage to be of value to both groups.

Different institutions may also bring their own fundamental sets of values to the assessment. One institution may have a strong emphasis on equity, for example, and be especially concerned about how effectively public services are reaching the poorest groups. Another may be primarily concerned with examining the incidence of corruption, perhaps because of its relevance to the domestic climate for private investment.

Finally, the same institution may need to apply the framework in significantly different ways depending on the specific circumstances of the country in question. In a highly authoritarian country, for example, in which public comment that departs from the ideology of the ruling party risks being treated as subversive, the questions that are relevant to ask will be different from those one might raise in a multiparty setting where civil society groups are already highly active in commenting publicly on multiple aspects of policy and administration.

There is thus no single prescribed way to apply the analytical approaches described in earlier chapters. In this sense, the framework that this book—and this chapter—offers does not represent a *blueprint* so much as a *toolkit*, with a series of elements each of which can help to generate questions that may be helpful in at least some country settings.

That said, it may be reasonable to expect that common elements of a relatively broad-based country assessment will include the following:

—An evaluation of the *outcomes from the current system*: how well do current governance arrangements meet reasonable expectations of government policies and services that are broadly efficient, honest, and equitable?

—An understanding of *the key elements in the relationships and processes* that lead to these outcomes, including the functioning of the political system, administrative norms (including the role of public sector watchdogs), and the nature of interactions between civil society actors and the state

—A sense of *potential avenues for improvement,* including the substantive content of desirable reforms and a view on the practical and political feasibility of possible strategies for their achievement

Based on these elements, this chapter presents some of the major issues that may arise in undertaking a country-level assessment, with the understanding that not all analysts will necessarily find it relevant to pick up all of the elements discussed here in all country settings.

Getting Started—Mining Readily Available Data

Before original work is started at the country level, it will make sense for the analyst first to mine readily available sources of information on governance in the country concerned. A useful first exercise may be to review the country's ratings in some of the growing number of cross-country ratings exercises.

Standardized Governance Indicators

A number of international sources provide comparative country indexes of one or more aspects of governance. In some cases, different indexes may not be entirely independent of each other, as some of these agencies prepare composite indexes that use other groups' ratings as their raw data. Nonetheless, while it would thus be misleading to treat all of the different indexes as strictly independent observations, the analyst who reviews a reasonable number of the better-established indexes should be able to obtain at least an impressionistic sense of the country conditions to be expected.

The annual Transparency International (TI) Corruption Perceptions Index, first issued in 1995, is among the best-known indexes. The TI analysts compile the index from underlying survey results provided by as many as a dozen different institutions. As its title suggests, the index reflects the *perceptions* of various groups polled, who are composed mainly of business executives or the staff of international agencies.[1]

Press coverage of the TI index often focuses on the "league table" nature of the listings—which countries moved up or down, relative to their peers. In view of the sometimes small differences in scoring that separate countries in the league, though, the analyst would be better advised to look first at a country's absolute score to see roughly where perceptions place its vulnerability to corruption at the present time. This may be supplemented by, first, considering whether the score has moved significantly over time in either a consistently positive or consistently negative direction and, second, comparing it with otherwise similar countries—regional neighbors, for example, or nonregional peers at similar levels of economic development. TI provides estimated confidence intervals for each of its country ratings, which provides a better context for interpreting the individual scores.

Another NGO undertaking country-level assessments is Global Integrity. This group emphasizes that, unlike TI, for example, it does not rely on polls but on the work of field-based experts who provide answers to a set of standardized factual questions. It also parts company with TI by declining to publish a global table. So far, Global Integrity covers a smaller number of countries than TI (43 compared with TI's 180).[2]

Among other important cross-country sources that analysts will want to review is the World Bank's Worldwide Governance Indicators (WGI), which are composed of a suite of metrics covering six aspects of governance: voice and accountability, political stability and absence of violence, government effectiveness, regulatory quality, rule of law, and control of corruption.[3] Digging as far as possible into the individual subcomponents of the indicators for each country may help identify particular areas of weakness.

A different perspective is provided by Freedom House, an NGO based in the United States with an independent board and management (though with significant U.S. government funding), which since 1972 has been issuing its Freedom in the World surveys. These surveys assess political rights (this part of the analysis is based on the responses to ten specific questions) and civil liberties (based on fifteen separate questions). As with the WGI dataset, there is more to be learned by digging into the individual elements of the assessment, and the accompanying country essays, than by focusing exclusively on the headline country ratings. In addition, while freedom of expression is among the elements factored into the Freedom in the World index, since 1980 Freedom House has also issued a more specific Freedom of the Press survey.[4]

The above organizations by no means exhaust the range of agencies providing cross-country governance indicators. At a more disaggregated level, subsequent sections of this chapter will refer to additional sources of country-level information on more specific aspects of governance.

Social and Economic Indicators

Aside from cross-country indexes that aim specifically to assess governance standards directly, it is worth emphasizing that cross-country sources can also be of value more indirectly, in helping to provide an economic and social context for the assessment of governance.

Standardized datasets, such as the World Bank's World Development Indicators, can help support a governance assessment in at least two ways.[5] First, the absolute level of aggregate indicators like per capita GDP can provide some guidance in establishing a country's overall level of development, including helping situate it among potential comparator countries in benchmarking exercises.

But at least as important, economic and social data can also provide a sense of how well the country (and by implication the government) is performing on behalf of the citizens. These types of data include not just the overall rate of economic growth but also measures of distribution, such as the Gini coefficient. These economic measures should also be supplemented by social indicators such as health and education indicators. This aspect is picked up in more detail in the subsequent section entitled "How Well Does the Government Serve the People?"

Political Systems

In launching more detailed work on a country governance assessment, it may make sense to start by reviewing the broad contours of the country's political system. At least in extreme cases, differences between country political systems can represent the single most important factor in establishing the overall scope for improving standards of governance and the channels through which it may be feasible to work for such improvements, including the potential role for initiatives by nongovernmental players in civil society.

Analysts have proposed different breakdowns of types of political systems, such as the possible fourfold (or fivefold) classification of political systems that was discussed earlier and that seeks to assign countries to one or other of the categories of liberal democracy, electoral democracy, electoral authoritarian, and closed authoritarian, with a possible additional category of failing or conflict-ridden states. Although these archetypes may provide useful points of reference, the challenge for the analyst is not to agonize over which of these categories a country most resembles but to grasp some of the essential points of how the system in the country in question actually functions. For present purposes, a multidimensional model may be of value, which compares systems along three axes:

—Executive power (the degree to which power is concentrated in the hands of a few and especially in the head of state)

—Citizen control (the degree to which the voice of citizens in public discourse and votes at the ballot box are taken seriously and influence outcomes)

—Institutionality (the degree to which duly adopted laws, rights, and practices are maintained and respected)

In turn, among the most important questions that emerge from this three-dimensional model are the following:

—What is the ability of other branches of government (the legislature and the judiciary) to restrain the executive?

—How far do civil society players, including NGOs and the media, enjoy the political space to play an autonomous role in monitoring and commenting on governance issues?

—To what extent does the rule of law offer protection from the potentially arbitrary behavior of those in power?

Those are among the main questions that need to be posed in the course of an assessment of country governance. To make a start in reviewing the issues involved, the rest of this section looks at the role of elections, the legislature, and the judiciary.

Role of Elections

Elections can potentially give a country's electors, in their role as principals, a voice in determining the future direction of the country and, more specifically, the power to change the agents who serve in the congress and who form the executive. The contestability of power is the central element in a population's ability to hold its rulers accountable. How efficiently do actual elections in a specific country allow the people to express their views and change their rulers?

In extreme cases, elections may be rendered mere formalities by a ruling party that allows only a single candidate for each position. Beyond this extreme, there are variations of systems in which elections do not translate into a realistic possibility of removing the ruling party from power, although some of the features of a multiparty democracy are present. Examples might include Mexico during the long period of the PRI's domination or either Russia or South Africa today. In some cases of this kind, a willingness to rig vote counts if needed—combined with overt intimidation—may be part of the mechanism, but in others this may prove unnecessary in view of the ruling group's ability to dominate communications media or to take advantage of national symbols or ethnic identities or both. Even within systems governed de facto by a single ruling party, though, voters may have some chance to cast a protest vote while some elements of pluralism may be found—for example, in contests between different wings of the ruling party for positions of power.

The way electors approach the voting process can also affect the clarity of the signals they transmit. If voters are accustomed to voting overwhelmingly on the basis of ethnic, religious, or other cultural identities, then voting will be largely neutralized as a means of signaling approval or disapproval of the actual conduct of government, or holding those in power genuinely accountable.

In addition, the mechanics of voting systems also may have a significant impact on how efficiently the signals sent by the electorate's votes actually get transmitted. For example,

—the drawing of constituency boundaries may advantage one group over another, even in the absence of deliberate gerrymandering—it is common, for example, for sparsely populated rural areas to be overrepresented in national legislatures relative to urban areas;

—first-past-the-post, constituency-based voting systems may suppress the emergence of new parties unless these parties are regionally based;

—in multiparty (as distinct from two-party) presidential systems that lack a second round of voting, a candidate may sometimes be elected to supreme office with only a relatively modest share of the total popular vote.

Role of Legislature

Legislative branches (parliaments and congresses) play roles in governance that can vary anywhere from assertively holding the executive accountable (through such mechanisms as the power of the purse and the power to undertake public investigations of executive conduct) to serving as little more than a rubber stamp for the ruling party. Where a country fits on this spectrum will reflect both the theory of constitutional provisions and the hard facts of party power.

Constitutional provisions in many parliamentary systems, such as those based on the Westminster model, give the legislature the authority, through a simple majority vote of no confidence, to oust a prime minister from office. Presidential models may also vest the ultimate power to dismiss the head of state in the congress, though typically only after meeting more exceptional requirements. (The U.S. Constitution, for example, requires the House of

Representatives to bring in Articles of Impeachment, followed by a conviction by a two-thirds majority in a trial in the Senate.)

Legislatures are typically responsible for approving new laws. There may, however, be variations in how far the congress itself, as opposed to the executive, can actually initiate new legislation. In authoritarian states, but also in some developing countries that fall well short of a fully authoritarian model, the executive may also in practice be able to appropriate much of the authority to legislate by the use of varying forms of unilateral directives, proclamations, and regulations, especially if it is relatively easy to declare a state of emergency.

Legislatures are typically vested with some degree of authority over the government budget—at a minimum, they are usually required to give at least formal approval to some form of government budget on an ex ante basis. They may also possess authority to monitor and investigate the executive's performance ex post, in budgetary and other areas. Where legislatures have the ability to hold public hearings, with witnesses legally required to attend, this can provide a powerful weapon to draw public attention to possible deficiencies in executive performance.

A subsequent section reviews in more detail some of the issues that can arise in the design and functioning of the budget process. Process issues, including, for example, the timeliness and completeness of budget submissions, can play an important role in defining the scope for effective review by the legislature (and possibly by civil society groups).

Another important element in the ability of a congress to hold the executive accountable is the resources that are allocated to the congress for its own staffing, the staffing of key committees being a critical factor. Given the huge bureaucracy available to the executive, members of congress require adequate numbers of qualified staff working on their behalf to undertake the type of research that is needed to dig below the surface of executive presentations. Providing improved resources to parliamentary committees has been an important element in reforms to strengthen their ability to hold the executive accountable, in settings ranging from the United Kingdom to a number of developing countries.

In some cases, though, at least as important a factor in the quality of congressional oversight may be the nature of the party system. When a single ruling party totally dominates the congress, there is an obvious risk that procedures will in practice be shaped to accomplish the executive's aims, including pushing through its legislation and its budget, rather than encouraging serious substantive review. On the other side of the aisle, when a reasonably stable and disciplined opposition bloc exists (which may hold a realistic prospect of gaining power), an incentive may exist for some opposition members to invest their time in developing the technical expertise needed to undertake serious review of legislative or budget issues. By contrast, in cases of fragmented party systems, in which loyalties are shifting, largely personalized, and often driven by patronage considerations, members of congress may see little payoff in spending their time and effort on the apparently mundane workload of a specialized committee.

Role of Judiciary

The role of the judiciary in governance is subject to considerable variation. At the highest level, many countries with written constitutions (including those broadly following the U.S. model) assign the judiciary the authority to disallow actions of either of the other two branches as unconstitutional (the Westminster model, by contrast, does not allow the judicial branch to overturn legislation duly adopted by parliament).

In practice, the ability of courts, including supreme courts, to act as effective checks on the other branches of government depends on the extent to which their independence is safeguarded. How are judges appointed? How much security of tenure do they enjoy? How easy is it to remove a judge from office, and upon what grounds—and by whom—can this be done? How protected are the budgets needed to operate the judicial system?

The level of efficiency and honesty of the courts can also have important direct impacts on the quality of governance experienced by the general population and on the investment climate (since entrepreneurs need efficient, honest courts to enforce contracts). In many countries, however, the efficiency and honesty of the courts are compromised by corruption within the judiciary itself.

A detailed report on corruption and judicial systems was published by Transparency International as the 2007 edition of its annual *Global Corruption Report.*[6] The report includes country reports on judicial corruption for thirty-five countries, making it a potentially useful source of country-level information for governance assessments.

More generally, TI finds that, in spite of several decades of reform efforts, judicial corruption remains disturbingly widespread. Across countries, "indicators of judicial corruption map neatly onto broader measures of corruption: judiciaries that suffer from systematic corruption are generally found in societies where corruption is rampant across the public sector." Two principal types of corruption are identified:

—*Political interference in judicial processes.* "A pliable judiciary," according to TI, "provides 'legal' protection to those in power for dubious or illegal strategies such as embezzlement, nepotism, crony privatizations, or political decisions that might otherwise encounter resistance in the legislature or from the media."

—*Bribery.* Bribery may be encountered at any level of the judicial system. Bribes may be demanded to decide a case in a specific way, or to decide it at all, or alternatively to delay a decision or "lose" a file.

In discussing systemic aspects of judicial sectors where problems can arise, TI points especially at

—judicial appointments, including failure to appoint judges on merit;

—terms and conditions, including poor salaries, but also unfair processes for promotion and transfer;

—accountability and discipline, including arrangements for the removal of judges (which may be misused to get rid of judges who display inconvenient independence and integrity);

—transparency, including opaque processes that prevent the media and civil society from monitoring court activity and exposing judicial corruption.[7]

In outlining approaches to the effective reform of corruption-plagued judicial systems, TI points to the need for a balance in matters of judicial independence. Judges need sufficient protection from outside interference with their work to enable them to exercise independence from the executive, but unqualified independence risks becoming a shield for corrupt judges.

Greater transparency, TI suggests, is an important element in the promotion of judicial accountability, including such measures as consultation with civil society over judicial appointments. Also recommended is the removal of artificial barriers to objective media coverage of court proceedings and possible instances of judicial corruption, such as "laws that criminalize defamation or give judges discretion to award crippling compensation in libel cases [and that] inhibit the media from investigating and reporting suspected criminality."

Administrative Systems

Most members of the public have little direct contact with politicians or judges. At the grass roots, the interface between government and the public is far more likely to consist of members of the civil service. The civil service is the main body of *agents* that are hired to serve the *principals,* who are the general population. How well do the incentive systems facing bureaucrats operate to align their actions with the public interest in good governance?

Civil Service

To answer this question for a specific country calls for an understanding of the processes that govern the hiring and firing of public officials as well as their assignment and possible promotion, the security of tenure they may enjoy, and the circumstances under which they may be subject to disciplinary action for misconduct. As with many other issues to be addressed in a governance assessment, the answers to these questions may require awareness of the official rules on the books and also of the practical culture of the "way things are really done."

In principle, two polar approaches apply to the recruitment and management of public officials. A *professionalized* (and avowedly politically neutral) service sets out to hire on meritocratic principles, for example through civil service examinations, and to promote according to demonstrated performance on the job. Subject to satisfactory performance, members enjoy a high degree of security of tenure and, in particular, continue to serve under administrations of different party backgrounds. This is the approach typically followed by countries that have adopted the Westminster model. It is also, for example, the model operated in Chile.

By contrast, in a *politicized* or patronage-based system, as for example in the United States, presidents, cabinet ministers, or governors hire many at least of the more senior officials who will work under them, and do so with due attention to their partisan political affiliation and loyalty. In patronage-based systems, the officials concerned typically would be expected to give up their position when the party (or the specific politician) that appointed them leaves office. Many real-world systems combine elements of both approaches: the professionalized and the politicized—the main difference between systems being the proportion of officials hired on one or the other basis.

Both approaches offer mechanisms that, if conscientiously applied, can create incentives for efficient and accountable government. The official in a professionalized system may partake in a shared sense among peers of what constitutes appropriate professional conduct (*sideways signals*) and is also potentially subject to sanction for infractions of discipline (*top-down signals*). The official in a politicized system may feel loyalty to a different set of norms—those upheld by the official's party. Nonetheless, to the extent that the official holds office only at the pleasure of senior officials of his or her party, any conduct that brings the party into bad repute may lead more or less to instant repercussions.

The above discussion assumes that the system, whether professionalized or politicized, is being run effectively, with strong flows of information on performance flowing up to those at or near the top, who are expected to take the lead responsibility for maintaining incentives and performance. If, for whatever reason, information does not flow effectively, or if those in senior positions show a lack of commitment to maintaining effective service—possibly because they feel little political pressure themselves from weak political signals and may be pursuing their personal interests in corrupt and possibly nepotistic dealings—then either model of system can in practice cease to serve the public good.

Decentralization

Over recent years, many developing countries around the world have carried out an extensive decentralization of key government functions. In Latin America, for example, the extent of decentralization of responsibility for most spending on basic health and education services and infrastructure facilities from central ministries to (frequently elected) governors, mayors, and councils has been so sweeping that one author categorized it as a "quiet revolution."[8]

Decentralization may create the possibility that the government becomes closer to the people—as exemplified, for example, by Porto Alegre in Brazil and its participatory budget process. But decentralization per se is no guarantee of transparency or accountability or of the efficient or equitable delivery of services to the population. Instead, decentralization may transfer many of the same questions this book has been raising about principal-agent relations, the role of special interests, and the extent of transparency from the national stage to a new venue, that of multiple local administrations all across developing countries.

There are a number of reasons for concern about the quality of governance at the local level. Particularly in rural areas, local society—and hence local government—may be dominated by large landowners or other traditional elites. Particularly in countries where political divides largely follow regional or ethnic lines, local political life may often be dominated by a single party. In small communities, where "everyone knows everyone," transactions between local government officials and potential contractors may be colored by long-standing personal ties. These settings may also be less hospitable than is a national capital to independent voices that might raise unwelcome questions over the conduct of public business by the local elite, possibly making it harder to sustain a genuinely independent press or other watchdog functions, such as those performed by independent monitoring organizations (IMOs).

Despite these potential hurdles, this book has argued that the role of local government in providing key services such as education and health has become so important that it cannot be ignored in reviewing key country-level governance issues. In considering priorities for intervention, a question that may arise is how to come at these issues first, from the top down or from the bottom up? One possible role for top-down intervention may be to promote the use of public expenditure tracking surveys (PETS) in a representative sample of areas to understand the extent of leakages when funds flow from the center to the local level. This can help dramatize the issue at the national level, thereby creating an opening for nationally based CSOs to push for systemwide policies of greater transparency over financial transfers.

However, top-down actions ideally should be complemented by a bottom-up approach: the mobilization of civil society at the local level to help improve the monitoring of local government. Despite the obstacles discussed earlier, CSOs may be able to create alliances at the local level, for example, with local religious groups; local media; and, especially in areas where local politics is genuinely competitive, with political figures willing to challenge potential abuses of power. These are useful analytical approaches that can be applied at the local level, such as benchmarking unit costs across neighboring jurisdictions so as to name and shame local governments that are paying inordinate amounts for standardized items compared with what their peers are paying.

Issues with the Fiduciary System

This section reviews the institutions and procedures within government that, if they are operating effectively, are designed specifically to promote efficient and accountable government. The section starts by examining procedures in such areas as budgeting and other aspects of public financial management and then the public procurement function. It then turns to a range of institutions intended to serve as public watchdogs. Finally, note is taken of the special issues that arise in connection with revenues from natural resource sectors, which often are perceived as especially vulnerable to misappropriation.

Budget Processes

The subject of government budgeting may sound dry and technical, but it is "where the rubber meets the road" in the sense that a central concern—arguably *the* central concern—in evaluating systems of governance is just how public resources are used. In a highly functional system of accountable governance, decisions about the future allocation of public resources would reflect careful and informed discussions over alternative options. The process of budget formation would be sufficiently transparent to allow for participation and awareness on the part of congressional opponents of the administration, the media, and representatives of civil society. In turn, the actual implementation of spending would be monitored with care and expected to be in line with what was decided in advance, unless explicit decisions were taken to change allocations. Detailed records would be kept that would permit ex post review to ensure that money was spent as appropriated and to analyze whether program design could be made more effective in future.

This description of an effective system conveys, by implication, clues to many of the things that can go wrong in budget systems that fall short. Budget decisions may be made largely behind closed doors and be based primarily on bureaucratic inertia (whereby agencies generally expect to receive last year's budget plus x percent) rather than on a serious substantive review of public priorities and the lessons of experience. In these cases of closed-off budget decisionmaking, generally only restricted information would be available, and congressional review would prove perfunctory (see the discussion on the role of the congress, above). Actual spending would be related only loosely to congressional appropriations, with the bureaucracy enjoying broad latitude to switch spending without further public consultation. Records may be kept in ways that make meaningful ex post review difficult if not impossible.

Specific concerns about budget processes include the following:

—Incomplete coverage of many official budgets, with significant areas of spending (and revenue) falling off-budget

—Expenditure categories that are uninformative because institutional boundaries are followed rather than substantive functional classifications or because definitions are adhered to that are obsolete or inconsistent

—Budget documents that are released to the congress so late in the year such that insufficient time is allowed for meaningful review that could actually influence allocations and, similarly, frequent delays in the availability of audited accounts: in this regard, the OECD has published guidelines for the timing of successive stages of government budgets

—Limitations to the power of congress to amend the budget submitted by the administration: only in about a quarter of countries does the congress have unrestricted power of reallocation

—Possible prevalence of earmarking of revenues automatically to specific purposes, which does not allow for transparent review of changing priorities

—Tendency of budget allocations to provide relatively generously for certain categories of expenditure (wages and salaries in general or curative services in health) while shortchanging others (supplies, maintenance, capital investment, or preventive services in health)

—Limitations of the right of the public to access information on the public budget: in a majority of countries, no public right of access to the budget exists and, in two out of five countries, the public lacks access to audited government financial statements

—Failure to publish full data on public debt, with only one in five countries providing significant information on contingent liabilities

Among the most serious deficits, three-quarters of governments provide little if anything in the way of ex ante performance indicators for different public programs. Close connections are not generally made between statements of government strategy on the one hand and the elements in the budget intended to realize the strategy on the other. Likewise, most governments provide nothing or almost nothing in the way of substantive ex post review of actual performance.

This book sees major potential for locally based civil society groups to play an important role in campaigning for improved budget transparency in individual countries. Independent monitoring organizations can press governments to release more information and to release it in more user-friendly formats. IMOs can also make use of information on budgets to promote greater public awareness and debate on the allocation of public resources—the extent to which government funds are allocated equitably between different elements in society, are used transparently and efficiently to promote agreed social goals, and so on.

The International Budget Partnership (IBP) is a decade-old international project that seeks to support IMOs in developing and transition countries in their efforts to promote greater budget transparency and more open debate over the equity of public spending. The IBP has produced a variety of training manuals on budget analysis designed for CSO use, and it also provides training courses, technical assistance, and funding to country-based CSOs engaging in budget analysis.

To provide a standardized indicator of budget openness across countries, the IBP has developed a comparative measuring tool, the Open Budget Index, and has worked with locally based CSOs to apply this methodology in approximately sixty countries so far. The summary evaluations assign countries to one of five groups, ranging from "provides extensive information to citizens" to "provides scant or no information to citizens."[9] Additional sources of information on country-level financial management are the World Bank's periodic Country Financial Accountability Assessments, which are available to the public.

Procurement

Government procurement is notoriously one of the main channels through which public resources find their way illegitimately into private pockets. Large infrastructure projects have a particularly bad reputation in this respect, although contracts for aircraft and weapons systems may have at least as unsavory a history. In all of these cases, large sums of money may change hands in a single transaction. There are also often enough technical complications in the nature of the product that at least a superficial cover story can be constructed to justify an apparently illogical contract award based on vague qualitative differences among the different bidders.

For any government that genuinely wishes to avoid malpractice in public procurement, there are various precautions that can be taken in the design of bidding procedures to make manipulation more difficult. First and foremost is to require some form of competition for any contract of any consequence as opposed to single-source procurement, which almost invites abuse. Beyond this, governments are well advised to insist on such safeguards as careful ex ante specification of the products and services to be supplied, advance publication of bid evaluation criteria, public bid openings, and so on. The major multilateral development banks, such as the World Bank, have spent decades refining standardized procedures for international or local competitive bidding; what *should* be done in the way of bid design is in most cases quite well understood. In many systems, however, political leaders or senior officials hold the well-founded belief that they can manipulate the award of a large contract to their own benefit without a high likelihood of detection and punishment.

Where there is an effective will to reform the system among top leaders, procedures can be reformed to incorporate the safeguards discussed above. Public watchdog agencies may need to be reinforced (see below). Better information can also prove to be, as Justice Louis Brandeis described the benefits of publicity, the "best disinfectant." At present, most countries lack centralized repositories of procurement information prepared according to transparent, standardized criteria that would make it easy for monitors, whether in the public sector or within civil society, to analyze the data to identify apparent anomalies. In this sphere, as in several others, there is potentially a double role for civil society organizations to make use of whatever information is currently available (from whatever source) to try to highlight likely abuses, while simultaneously campaigning for the longer-term goal of greatly improved public information systems on government procurement that are accurate, timely, complete, and user-friendly. Among public sources of information on country-level procurement issues are the World Bank's periodic Country Procurement Assessment Reports.

Public Watchdogs

Most systems of public administration include a variety of institutions and officials whose official raison d'être is to protect the public interest from possible failings or misconduct on the part of others in the administration. Virtually every system is equipped with public audit agencies, including a supreme audit institution. There may also be inspectors general for specific agencies. Over recent decades, a growing number of countries have also copied the initially Scandinavian concept of the ombudsman, an official with a fairly wide mandate to investigate complaints about government conduct brought by members of the public.

One important distinction between different categories of watchdogs across countries is the question of from whom they derive their authority and to whom they are answerable. In particular, some watchdogs form part of the executive branch, while others act as arms of the legislature. This factor is among the many that may affect the degree of independence they may enjoy.

A healthy range of watchdog agencies, whose independence is respected and which have the resources needed to do their job effectively, constitutes one important element in an effectively functioning system of governance. Such watchdogs can also provide a highly valuable source of information for civil society groups on the functioning of the public sector—information that the CSOs may then be able to analyze further or use to raise public awareness of governance problems.

By contrast, the two main ways in which watchdogs may fall short of their potential are typically either a lack of effective operational independence or a lack of resources (whether funds, qualified staff, or access to information). Auditors in some countries lack the formal autonomy to decide which activities to audit. Auditors also frequently spend so much of their time on routine compliance work that they lack the resources to undertake more strategic investigations of systematically wasteful programs or higher-level misconduct.

Natural Resource Revenues

Public revenues from certain natural resource sectors, especially oil, gas, and minerals, are frequently more subject to misappropriation by political and official elites than are other forms of government revenues. Such revenues tend to be large in overall amounts and also highly concentrated. One or a handful of big producers in a country may account for large absolute sums, which also may well represent a high proportion of total government revenues.[10] As a high proportion of total earnings tends to consist of economic rent over and above the costs of production, the revenues represent easy money and invite secret deals between the producing companies and a small number of officials at the top of the country's political system. In such cases oil earnings would not be transparently accounted for within the national budget but would be subject to special arrangements that obscure the total amounts involved and their destination.

Because the amounts of money are so large for many countries, the stakes can be very high for all concerned. A number of international civil society networks have taken up the issue and are conducting campaigns to urge the multinational companies concerned to "publish what you pay" while also supporting national civil society coalitions in their own efforts to press for transparency within government accounts. A number of developed country governments and major international corporations have recently made public declarations of support for greater transparency in this area.[11]

How Well Does the Government Serve the People?

It is said that "the proof of the pudding lies in the eating," and this is true of governance too. A fundamental test of any system of government—and of any specific administration—is how well the country's economy and public services work on behalf of the people.

A country governance assessment thus should include efforts to examine how well the system delivers to the average citizen. This can be supplemented with useful information by asking more specifically about those who labor under some form of potential disadvantage, such as women; the elderly; those living in remote or rural areas; those belonging to traditionally less-favored ethnic, linguistic, or religious groups; those living with a disability; and so on.

A first step in a country governance assessment is to review the main economic and social data that are published on a regular basis by the national statistical agency and international sources such as the UN or the World Bank's

World Development Indicators. The effectiveness of the way the economy has been managed in overall terms may be gauged by standard indicators such as the average medium-term growth of per capita GDP and trends in absolute and relative poverty indicators. Distribution may also be measured using the Gini coefficient, although this requires significant survey data to estimate accurately, and as such it may be available only for years in which surveys were undertaken.

Economic data should be supplemented by social indicators, such as life expectancy and maternal and infant mortality rates as well as literacy rates and other measures of educational progress. It is usually possible to obtain data on the proportion of children registered in school at various levels (primary and secondary), and often these data are also broken down by gender—an important point since in some societies girls are much less likely to be in school. However, it is also desirable to obtain data on actual student learning achievement, which provides an indicator of the *quality* of the educational system—such as students' performance on standardized international tests such as the Programme for International Student Assessment, which sixty-five countries are planning to conduct in 2009.[12]

The value of all of these social and economic indicators to governance assessment will be enhanced by looking for trends over time in the country in question to see whether things are improving, stagnating, or deteriorating and by benchmarking the country's performance against broadly comparable countries in its region and income group. Breakdowns of the indicators, if available on a regional basis or for specific groups within the population (such as ethnic minorities), will cast light on how well the government has closed gaps between the more- and less-favored groups in the population.

It is highly desirable to be able to dig beyond these standardized indicators, by means of special surveys. Several types of analysis have shown promise in selected developing country settings.

Incidence studies seek to review which elements in society gain the most from key forms of public expenditure (the technique can also be extended to look at the revenue side of government and identify who pays the most in taxes). It is frequently found that even social programs that are broadly based, such as those in health and education, tend to favor the higher-income deciles, because of higher levels of spending in urban as opposed to rural areas and also concentration of spending in tertiary education or advanced city hospitals, for example, which typically are more heavily used by the more affluent and better-connected elements in the population. But even public pension programs turn out upon examination (for example, in much of Latin

America) to benefit primarily those in relatively high-income groups, such as senior government officials and formal workers in the private sector.

Public expenditure tracking surveys seek to identify the proportion of public funds voted for a specific program—for example, rural basic health care or education—that actually get through to the grassroots level at which patients are treated or children educated. In other words, PETS estimate leakages at different levels of the bureaucracy. Famous examples include studies of educational spending in Uganda and Kenya, which showed exceptionally high leakages and helped create pressure to stanch the losses. Actions taken in response to this pressure included initiating procedures for greater transparency of the allocations for each community.

Citizen report cards, which are an initiative from India, survey the public to estimate levels of satisfaction with the quality, honesty, timeliness, and responsiveness of grassroots government services. Indian NGOs have published the results of these surveys to make comparisons within peer groups and name and shame government units that fall short of satisfactory standards.

These types of surveys provide important raw material for country-level governance assessments. Where they have not yet been undertaken, a valuable role for a governance assessment would be to create pressure to carry such studies out.

The Media

The media, whether print, broadcast, or (increasingly) web-based, can potentially play an enormously important role in improving governance. They can do this first and foremost by playing their own traditional independent journalistic role but also—potentially—by developing new alliances with elements in civil society, including IMOs.

Perhaps most important, vibrant media can provide citizens with information relevant to carrying out their role as electors (principals deciding whether to hold their agents accountable to the point of changing them) in a better-informed way. But media coverage potentially can also highlight numerous other aspects of governance discussed in this book—publicizing debates on budgetary choices, for example, or pursuing investigations into government inefficiency or suspected cases of corruption.

In a study from 2000 that is, at least, suggestive of the significant role that can be played by a strong press, the Inter-American Development Bank compiled an index of government quality, comprising four elements derived from World Bank work on governance (the ability of government to enforce contracts and protect the lives and property of its citizens, the incidence of corruption, the efficiency of government in delivering public services, and the incidence of burdensome regulations on the economy). The study found that the single strongest explanatory variable for government quality was a country's per capita circulation of newspapers. The relationship held after controlling for per capita income. It also survived if the sample was restricted to either only developed or only developing countries.[13]

Constraints on Media Freedom

Clearly, it is not automatic that the media will make a significant positive contribution to more transparent and accountable government. It is easy to think of countries where the media form little more than a propaganda arm of the government. Even in countries where overt government censorship has ceased, journalists are sometimes quoted as saying that they learn to practice self-censorship by avoiding topics known to be politically sensitive to those in power.

Beyond this, in some countries where media control is highly concentrated, even if in private hands, there is concern that media owners will primarily pursue their own commercial interests, and perhaps they may settle into a cozy arrangement with the political leadership in which the media do not seriously rock the boat. Pluralism, a multiplicity of voices, provides some protection against this type of narrowing of the range of expression. This in turn serves as a reminder that among the most important dimensions of media freedom is the absence of artificial barriers to entry into media-related sectors (whether created by government regulations or by oligopolistic control).

To provide a starting point for a more detailed field-based assessment, a number of international groups monitor press freedom around the world. Freedom House has published its annual freedom of the press survey since 1980. In the organization's own words,

> Now covering 194 countries and territories, *Freedom of the Press: A Global Survey of Media Independence* provides numerical rankings and rates each country's media as "free," "partly free," or "not free." Country narratives examine the legal environment for the media, political pressures that influence reporting, and economic factors that affect access to information.[14]

Another group, Reporters without Borders, an international nonprofit network, likewise produces an annual worldwide press freedom index, accompanied by individual country reports. The organization also undertakes special investigations in countries in which particular threats to press freedom are feared.[15]

Strengthening Media Capacity—Scope for Collaboration with CSOs

Aside from external threats to media freedom, another important factor to consider is the actual capacity of individual media outlets and the journalists who work for them to research and report governance-related stories. Many newspapers and magazines operate on relatively tight budgets and cannot afford to invest large amounts of resources to develop the capability to report on what may appear to be relatively technical issues, such as details of the budget process. Television channels, operating on a national basis, may have larger overall resources, but they tend to be wary of departing from programming that readily appeals to a mass audience. In addition, in many developing countries, the typical reporter generally lacks an advanced educational background that would readily equip him or her to deal with economic or financial issues.

These considerations draw attention to the possibility for symbiosis between NGOs and think tanks functioning as IMOs, which have the ability to process information on governance issues, and elements in the media that potentially may be interested in carrying stories on governance questions but have limited ability to acquire and process relevant information by themselves. Such collaboration will require both sides to make an investment in collaboration, with the IMOs, in particular, needing to learn how to process and present their work in ways that the media can use.

In practical terms, this may require IMOs to give much higher priority to developing dissemination strategies for their work at an early stage—indeed, possibly designing their work programs from the outset with the view of how to promote their results to the media. Training IMO staff in media-related techniques, and designating some of their senior staff members as resources that the media can call at any time on specific issues, are approaches that have become widespread in recent years among think tanks in developed countries. In addition, IMOs in the developing world are starting to develop training courses for media staff on the substance of governance-related issues—an important investment in future collaboration.

Prioritizing Potential Interventions

Some agencies may wish to undertake a country governance assessment that will serve as an overall background to their country operations, but many are likely to use such an assessment to help them prioritize possible operational interventions. Although the framework provided here should be of value in developing such priorities, there is nothing in the framework that makes the process of prioritization automatic or mechanistic. A specific agency's priorities in country X will reflect its own identity—its overall modus operandi and values—as well as whatever it learns during the course of a country assessment. The framework does not substitute for the need for careful weighing of alternatives by the agency concerned, but hopefully it can offer alternatives that might otherwise not have been considered, as well as improve the understanding of the implications of some of the alternatives that would in any case have been on the menu.

A simple framework to help an organization think about the process of prioritization would pose two questions when the organization is considering various alternative actions:

—First, what is the nature and scale of the expected payoff in case the proposed intervention is successful? What value would the agency that is making the assessment place on this possible payoff?

—Second, what are the likely costs of the intervention and the anticipated probability of its success?

When it is considering the potential payoff to success, the agency could establish approximate orders of magnitude for some key variables. One possible route to quantification may be to make use of comparative data for comparable countries (or subnational regions) that are more successful in one way or another—for example, in getting more children into school, improving the supply of medications to rural health clinics, or achieving a more competitive bidding process for local public works. Other instances may lend themselves less to quantification—heroic assumptions might be needed to place a dollar value on the benefits from passing a Freedom of Information Act. That said, cross-country comparisons can provide a basis, for example, for suggesting the degree to which achieving better overall governance indicators might help to improve levels of investment and growth.

Survey data from local populations or from subsets that are of special interest could serve as another source of data to help in the prioritization of possible outcomes. Surveys that focus on ordinary citizens, or specifically on the poor, may help highlight the extent to which they are primarily concerned with the quality of their children's schools, lack of clean drinking water, or abusive conduct by the local police. Similarly, surveys of entrepreneurs may help identify the most important elements of governance that affect the investment climate.

Beyond these external elements, a particular agency's specific values are also likely to affect the weight it attaches to different outcomes. One agency may place a higher (or lower) value on one type of result, for example improved social indicators, compared with that of another, for example reduced corruption in the customs administration.

Mapping Interests and Identifying Potential Allies

The framework presented in this book may also assist in the assessment of the costs and probability of success of possible interventions. Mapping the interests involved, in particular, will identify those who may be potential allies and also, critically, those likely to oppose the change. For potentially high-payoff reforms, digging into the issue in more detail to get a sense of what the stakes are for both sides—and the levers of power and influence each may be able to pull—would lend added realism to the calculus of what is likely to be involved.

To prepare a country-level mapping of interests that is comprehensive is a highly labor-intensive process. It might be preferable to start with a more selective mapping. Although it may be possible, at least in broad terms, to identify some of the more important interest groups in the country, it needs to be borne in mind that the possible depth of interest by a particular group—and the alliances that it may be open to—may vary greatly depending on the type of policy questions that are on the table at any particular time. A particular industry or labor union may be a sleeping giant for 90 percent of the time but awake with a roar if issues specific to its own sector are under discussion. As such, it may make sense to have in mind a potential list of possible governance reforms as the background to a mapping of interests rather than trying to undertake the mapping in a vacuum.

An operational governance assessment should include at least a broad sketch of who the key players are in organized civil society, including groups that have already shown an interest—or strong potential—for engagement in governance issues, whether primarily on the analytical side or more on the mobilization and campaigning side. What are the issues these groups already care about? What connections might be made to other issues of importance? What are their existing resources and capabilities? What weak areas could be reinforced through well-designed interventions? These sorts of questions inter alia may help identify interventions in the way of institution-strengthening programs, which are much less likely to be contentious than would proposals for specific reforms in public policies.

When mapping out the potential for specific reform campaigns, an agency needs to ask what alliances might reform-minded elements in civil society be able to create—at least for individual campaigns of importance—with other elements in the country: The media? Professional societies? Reform-minded elements in politics? Government watchdogs or specific ministries? Ministries of finance, for example, worry a great deal about potentially wasteful expenditures on the part of "spending ministries" and, in some circumstances, may welcome greater involvement of civil society to improve transparency and accountability. Equally, are there important divisions within civil society—for example, along political, ethnic, or religious lines—that might create difficulty for different groups to work together?

Of particular interest in weighing potential alliances may be the identification of economic or social groups that see themselves as losing out from the current situation. Perhaps small businesses feel that opaque government procedures largely benefit their larger competitors. International firms might feel that domestic companies are better able to game the system (or vice versa). Neglected regions or ethnic groups may feel that greater transparency over inequitable spending patterns would aid their cause. And so on.

But a serious examination of the feasibility of a specific reform will need to include research not only into potential allies but also into those likely to oppose the reform. Which groups see themselves as benefiting from the status quo in this particular area? How much do these groups have at stake over the specific issue? Who are their natural allies? Which levers are they most likely to pull? How might they be outflanked and what types of public campaigns might likely swing public opinion behind the cause of reform?

It is a matter of judgment exactly how far a broad governance assessment should go in designing specific interventions in detail or in laying out specific campaigns to win broader support. Nonetheless, at least some broad sense of the potential feasibility of various recommendations and the implications of endeavoring to put them into practice will help give the assessment a greater degree of relevance for its users.

Notes

1. For information on sources and methodology, as well as specific country scores, see the TI webpage "CPI Table and Sources" (www.transparency.org/policy_research/surveys_indices/cpi).

2. For more information about Global Integrity and its projects visit its website (www.globalintegrity.org/index.cfm).

3. See the World Bank webpage Worldwide Governance Indicators: 1996–2007 (http://go.worldbank.org/ATJXPHZMH0).

4. For more information about these surveys, including methodology and country-specific scores, see the website of Freedom House (www.freedomhouse.org).

5. World Bank, *World Development Indicators* (Washington, annual).

6. Transparency International, *Global Corruption Report 2007: Corruption in Judicial Systems* (Cambridge University Press, 2007).

7. Transparency International, *Global Corruption Report 2007*.

8. Tim Campbell, *The Quiet Revolution: Decentralization and the Rise of Political Participation in Latin American Cities* (University of Pittsburgh Press, 2003).

9. See the Open Budget Initiative webpage "Open Budget Index 2006" for more information on the index and country rankings (www.openbudgetindex.org/Open BudgetIndex2006.pdf).

10. A central element in the so-called Dutch disease, which characterizes highly resource-rich countries, is that a high level of foreign exchange earnings from, for example, mineral development leads to an appreciation of the real exchange rate. This in turn chokes off exports from nonmineral sectors, making the country—and very often the government budget also—very highly dependent on mineral earnings.

11. For further details on the issues involved in transparent accounting for natural resource revenues and on civil society efforts to improve transparency, see, for example, the websites maintained by the Publish What You Pay coalition (www. publishwhatyoupay.org/), and the Revenue Watch Institute (www.revenuewatch.org/). Support for these efforts is also provided by the International Budget Partnership. A related initiative launched by the British government, and now supported by a number of governments, corporations, and other agencies, is the Extractive Industries Transparency Initiative.

12. For more information about this international test, visit OECD's website (www.pisa.oecd.org).

13. Inter-American Development Bank, *Development beyond Economics* (Washington, 2000), pp. 186-91.

14. For more information on the methodology, findings, and country reports, see the Freedom House website (www.freedomhouse.org).

15. See Reporters without Borders website for more information about the organization, its activities, and specific country reports (www.rsf.org).

APPENDIXES

Country Case Studies

VITUS AZEEM

A

Transparency and Accountability in Ghana's Budget Process

Historical Governance Context

After ten years of military rule, Ghana held democratic elections in 1992, which were won by the National Democratic Congress (NDC), led by Flight Lieutenant J. J. Rawlings, who had ruled until 1992 under the military regime. Since then, Ghana has been described as an oasis of peace and tranquility in a tumultuous region that has seen civil wars in several neighboring countries. The country has made steady progress toward consolidating and strengthening liberal democracy, having held three successful general elections and managed an orderly transfer of power in 2001 from the NDC to the New Patriotic Party (NPP), which has remained in power since then.[1] With the return of democratic rule, several freedoms were restored. The new government repealed two laws, the Criminal Libel Act and the Seditious Law, which expanded the frontiers of freedom and human rights and promoted transparency and accountability in society. The liberalization of the airwaves has led to a proliferation of media houses, with FM radio stations broadcasting and newspapers publishing freely.

Before this restoration of freedoms, civil society organizations and other nongovernmental organizations were mainly self-help, relief, and development-oriented groups working to assist government agencies to fulfill their

1. While this volume was being prepared for publication in January 2009, Ghana's election commission declared the opposition NDC candidate the victor in a tight race with the NPP for the presidency. (*Editor*).

113

social service obligations. However, by the mid-1990s, NGOs and CSOs experienced a major shift, focusing increasingly on campaigns and advocacy programs aimed at ensuring accountability, transparency, nondiscrimination and poverty-related issues that promote good governance, respect for human rights, and the delivery of the right level and quality of social services. These campaigns targeted government, public institutions, and elements of the private sector whose activities negatively affected the welfare of ordinary people.

However, a recent development that may inhibit the activities of CSOs, especially those engaged in advocacy work, is the issue of policy guidelines for NGOs and the introduction of a Trust Bill seeking to subject NGO activities to government control and trust laws.

Recent Developments

Over the past fifteen years, Ghana has achieved overall economic growth averaging almost 5 percent per year. The per capita GDP growth rate averaged 2.2 percent per year over same period. The GDP growth rate rose from 3.7 percent in 2000 to 6.2 percent in 2006. The rate of inflation fell from 21.3 percent in 2001 to about 11.8 percent in 2006.

The Ghana Living Standards Survey (GLSS 4) in 1998–99 showed that the incidence of overall poverty in Ghana fell from 52 percent of the population in 1991–92 to 40 percent in 1998–99, while extreme poverty declined from 37 percent to 27 percent during the same period. The GLSS 5 found that the poverty headcount declined further to 35 percent in 2003, with export farmers and private sector employees benefiting the most, while food crop farmers benefited the least. Poverty remained disproportionately concentrated in the savannah zone, that is, the country's three northern regions. The African Peer Review Mechanism, APRM, (2005) revealed that the quality and availability of health services was very low. Similarly, school enrollment and retention, especially in the three northern regions, remained low.

In 2001, Ghana decided to access the enhanced Heavily Indebted Poor Countries (HIPC) Initiative. The country faced an external debt of US$6.0 billion. While progressing with the HIPC process, Ghana adopted the Multi Donor Budget Support (MDBS) system of donor support in 2003, aimed at better coordinating donor support, though still relying heavily on the IMF's assessment of the country's economic performance. In May 2003, the IMF expressed satisfaction with Ghana's conduct of its macroeconomic policy and declared that the economy was on a steady growth path, fiscal discipline had been restored, and official reserves had exceeded targets. Ghana reached the HIPC completion point in 2004, enabling it to obtain substantial debt relief.

With the introduction of the Multilateral Debt Relief Initiative in 2005, the total debt relief under the two initiatives amounted to US$4,558 million in 2006.[2] Ghana was also selected to benefit from the Millennium Challenge Account, which earmarked a total of US$547 million over a five-year period for projects aimed at agricultural transformation and export expansion.

Ghana produced a poverty reduction strategy paper, the Ghana Poverty Reduction Strategy (GPRS I), covering the period from 2003 to 2005, that was designed to ensure that any debt relief savings went into programs that would benefit the poor and reduce poverty. The GPRS I focused on five main thematic areas: macroeconomic stability, production and gainful employment, human resource development, vulnerability and exclusion, and good governance. The second phase, the Growth and Poverty Reduction Strategy (GPRS II), covers the period from 2006 to 2009 and focuses on accelerating private sector–led growth and promoting vigorous human resource development and encouraging good governance and civic responsibility. The GPRS I did not assign any monitoring and evaluation role to civil society, but the GPRS II monitoring framework has recognized the important role of CSOs. Also, some donors, such as the World Bank and the U.K. Department for International Development, have encouraged, supported, and funded civil society groups engaged in the monitoring of poverty reduction expenditures and debt relief.

In 2003, Ghana made strong efforts to improve governance, transparency, and accountability; curb corruption; and ensure the efficient utilization of public resources, enacting the Internal Audit Agency Act, 2003 (Act 658); the Financial Administration Act, 2003 (Act 654); and the Public Procurement Act, 2003 (Act 663). An Office of Accountability was established under the presidency to check the compliance of political appointees with existing anti-corruption laws and standards of public ethics and integrity.[3] However, the work of the Office of Accountability has remained a closed activity. Ghana was one of the first countries to submit to the African Peer Review Mechanism, and the country's self-assessment was completed and submitted in March 2005. In 2006, the Whistleblower Act, 2006 (Act 720) was also enacted. However, public officials, on their assumption of office, still have to swear the Oath of Secrecy that restricts them as to what information they can release to the public. Moreover, a Freedom of Information (FOI) Bill, which was first drafted in 1999 to provide the legal framework for access to information, has not yet been enacted.

2. Information from IMF documents found at its website.
3. CDD-Ghana.

Diagnosis

Ghana's Constitution makes the executive solely responsible for the formulation and execution of the budget (Article 179). The bureaucracy, made up of the ministries, departments, and agencies (MDAs), under the supervision of the respective ministers (political appointees), performs these roles on behalf of the executive.

Principal Actors

The MDAs prepare the budget estimates for the year for consideration and approval by the cabinet. The Ministry of Finance and Economic Planning (MoFEP) coordinates their activities and lays the budget proposals before parliament. The executive is also responsible for the implementation of the approved budget. The Policy, Planning, Monitoring, and Evaluation Divisions (PPMED) of the MDAs plan and monitor the implementation of the budget.

The Parliament of Ghana is responsible for approving the budget as proposed by the executive and has oversight over the executive in the execution of the budget and other financial transactions, including the approval of loans. The constitution makes the parliament the only authority that can impose taxation in the country (Article 174) and the only authority that can authorize the withdrawal of public funds from the Consolidated Fund and any other funds, which in turn can only be created under the authority of the parliament (Article 178). In sum, all public expenditures must be authorized by the parliament. Similarly, Article 181 gives the parliament the power to authorize all international business and economic transactions, including loans from and to the government of Ghana. The Parliament of Ghana has performed these roles over the years, but its impacts are limited because of several constraints it faces.

The auditor-general is responsible for auditing the public accounts of Ghana and of all public offices and for reporting to parliament, drawing its attention to any irregularities in the accounts and any other matter found necessary. In practice, the office of the auditor-general performs its constitutional roles, although it faces several challenges, including overdue submissions of audit reports, and sometimes has to outsource some work to private firms because of limited capacity.

Civil society does not have any institutionalized role in the budget process. However, in 2005, the MoFEP called on civil society organizations and individual citizens to make submissions to the 2006 annual budget. Some submissions were made for potential inclusion in the 2006 and the 2007 budgets (the Budget Statements for the 2006 and 2007 financial years) by individual citizens, private business representatives, and civil society organizations.

Finally, the budget process in Ghana is heavily influenced by its development partners, which not only provide substantial resources, especially for the capital budget, but also make recommendations for government budget policies.

Relative Power Balance between Principal Actors (De Jure and De Facto)

The executive is the most powerful institution in Ghana's budget process, determining the sources of budget funds, the budget policies, and the proposed expenditure estimates. Parliament's amendment powers are limited to revising the executive's proposals downward or rejecting the proposals in their entirety. In practice, the parliament has always been dominated by the ruling party, making it most unlikely for it to totally reject the budget proposals. Thus the executive has always had its way, and parliament's role is often a mere formality. The APRM (2005) identified the limited ability of the parliament to perform its representative, legislative, and oversight functions as one of the serious challenges facing Ghana's democracy.[4]

All sectors of the economy in Ghana experience the influential role of donors in policymaking because the country depends on donor resources to fill the financing gap. Donor assistance is based on the IMF's assessment of the country's economic performance and of its implementation of structural reforms negotiated with the international financial institutions (IFIs). The APRM argued that two main challenges facing Ghana, weak internal capacity in economic management and heavy dependence on external resources for financing government development expenditure, compel the country to accept the IFIs' guidance and direction on macroeconomic programming. Thus IFIs and even bilateral donors are ranked above local research institutes, private sector institutions, and public sector groups as sources of inputs to policymaking and economic planning.

Interaction of Institutions in the Budget Process (Signals and Actions)

All interactions at the budget formulation stage have always been among the executive and its technocrats. The budget process starts with a circular from the MoFEP to the MDAs inviting estimates for the budget for the coming year. This circular provides deadlines as well as ceilings for the estimates.

---

4. African Peer Review Mechanism (APRM), *Country Review Report of the Republic of Ghana* (Midrand, South Africa: APRM Secretariat, 2005).

Following the introduction of the medium-term expenditure framework system of budgeting, there usually has been some training of the budget officers and other key players before the preparation of the budgets by the MDAs. Though not institutionalized, this formulation stage is in practice the stage during which other stakeholders, such as advocacy and special interest groups, traditional rulers, opinion leaders, and parliamentarians, can potentially engage the executive over the content of the budget. In the last two years, it has also been at this stage that the MoFEP has put advertisements in the newspapers calling on citizens and organized groups to make proposals for the budget.

After the MoFEP has collected and collated the budget estimates from the MDAs, hearings are held so that the MDAs have the opportunity to defend their proposals, which enables the MoFEP to prune them back in-line with the estimated available resources. The cabinet approves the budget estimates before they are laid before the parliament for debate and approval. In recent years, the MoFEP has announced a date for the laying of the budget before parliament about a week or two in advance. It is only on the day that the budget is laid before parliament that the members of the parliament get to know what is in the budget. During the debate, the ministries appear before the relevant parliamentary subcommittees to defend their proposals. The approval of the budget by the parliament is the signal to the executive that it can implement the budget. The only other time that the parliament interacts with the executive over the budget is when the parliament finds it necessary to invite a minister to answer questions on aspects of the implementation of the budget.

Critical Strong and Weak Links between the Actors

Ghana's 1992 Constitution requires the president to appoint the majority of cabinet ministers from among the members of parliament. Beyond this, the president usually also appoints many noncabinet ministers and even deputy ministers from parliament. Ghana has nearly ninety ministers and deputy ministers, and most of them are also members of the 230-member parliament. That means that a minister could preside over the preparation of a ministry's budget estimates, subsequently attend a cabinet meeting to approve them, and then go to parliament to debate and approve the budget. Thus, by the time the budget reaches the lawmaking body, it is more or less cut and dried. Moreover, the parliament over the last fifteen years has always been dominated by the president's ruling party, and party loyalty has always superseded national interest.

The only real influence that the parliament can have over the budget is, therefore, informal. Therefore any attempt to influence the budget by any stakeholder, including civil society and parliament, can only be achieved through interactions with the executive at the formulation stage. The ruling party can use its advantaged position to push budget policies or loan agreements through parliament and suppress parliament's oversight role, for example by blocking decisions on adverse findings by the auditor-general.

The auditor-general is responsible for performing part of parliament's oversight role on its behalf and reports periodically to the parliament. The reports are debated by the Public Accounts Committee, which makes recommendations to the full house for adoption. However, parliament has no power to enforce any of its recommendations, and thus enforcement depends on the goodwill of the executive. Unfortunately, there has not been any encouraging action by the executive on audit reports.

The relationship between Ghana's development partners (DPs) and the government clearly demonstrates the importance of these institutions in Ghana's economy and the budget process. All loan negotiations and policy decisions as well as performance assessments are done between the executive and DPs. Parliament plays no role at all in these negotiations except to endorse the agreements. CSOs are not involved in any negotiations with the DPs as well. However, a few CSO representatives have been invited to attend consultative group (CG) meetings. In recent times, it has been announced to the public when donors are going to meet government for negotiations, the MDBS reviews, and CG meetings.

Ghana's Constitution provides for a system of local government and administration, and the decentralization of government involves local authority structures called, respectively, metropolitan, municipal, and district assemblies (MMDAs). However, decentralization has been mainly administrative in nature, as fiscal and political decentralization has been "weak, demobilized, unresponsive and ineffective," hindering participation in decisionmaking, accountability, and transparency in social service delivery at the lower levels of government.[5]

Role of Civil Society

Citizens play various roles through intermediaries, such as the media, NGOs and civil society organizations, and private sector and special interest groups. Civil society budget activists such as the Centre for Budget Advocacy (CBA) of the Integrated Social Development Centre, the Social Enterprise Development Foundation of West Africa (SEND Foundation), and the Institute for

5. APRM (2005).

Democratic Governance (IDEG) have sought to strengthen the linkages between the rulers and the citizens and to influence the budget process through budget analysis, advocacy, and submission of inputs based on information collated from their analyses and public forums, as well as the monitoring of budget execution and tracking of resource flows. However, goodwill and political commitment on the part of the government play a very important role in determining the success of civil society work in the budget process.

CSOs need to build their capacities and equip themselves with the necessary knowledge and skills in advocacy in their areas of interest. Civil society itself needs to be more aware of its roles and responsibilities vis-à-vis basic human rights, to demand these rights, and to play the appropriate roles in ensuring that they are met. In addition, CSOs also need to build the capacities of other stakeholders and sensitize them, especially the media, on the need for transparency and accountability. CSOs have to disseminate information and research findings on the budget process, which in turn will lend credence and support to the demand that civil society have a role in the budget process.

Second, coalition building is essential for successful CSO engagement and advocacy with the executive. Civil society must, therefore, organize itself into pressure groups, demand a role in the budget process, and play it effectively. It can also demand the enactment and enforcement of transparency and anti-corruption legislation that provides for access to relevant information needed to improve accountability and curb corruption. Civil society should also continue and expand the tracking of resource flows and the monitoring of service providers' performance with the objective of improving effectiveness and efficiency in service delivery. The results of these tracking exercises should be used to engage the appropriate authorities and demand policy reforms in public expenditures. CSOs can also engage in the monitoring of elections, and discourage vote buying and other unfair means of influencing the electorate.

Examples of Successful CSO Engagement

Since 2000, civil society organizations have undertaken various activities aimed at influencing the budget process and shaping public expenditure policy in Ghana through advocacy and engagement with the government. These activities include budget policy analyses and advocacy, training and sensitization of public officials and citizens, monitoring of budget implementation and tracking of budgetary resource flows, facilitation of community assessments of service delivery, and surveys on transparency and corruption. These activities are aimed at bringing about equitable budgetary allocations, efficient disbursement and utilization of resources and the avoidance of wastage, and improved transparency and accountability from public officeholders.

The CBA's budget analyses, press conferences, and public forums on the budget and other economic policies, as well as its budget training workshops, have generated public interest and activism in the budget process and, hence, influenced budget and public expenditure policy. The IDEG-led initiative that enabled civil society groups to make inputs into the GPRS II, the 2007 budget, and the CG meeting in 2007 are examples of civil society efforts to shape public expenditure policies. The SEND Foundation's HIPC Watch project's tracking of HIPC funds, the Ghana National Education Campaign Coalition and the Northern Network for Education and Development's education expenditure tracking exercises, and the Institute for Policy Alternatives–led monitoring exercises can be cited as successful CSO engagement within the governance structure in shaping public expenditure policy for better outcomes. These groups have engaged government with their findings and recommendations. Think tanks, such as the Centre for Policy Analysis, Institute of Economic Affairs, and Institute of Statistical, Social, and Economic Research, have carried out budget analyses and annual assessments of the economy over the years, exposing policy gaps and making recommendations to address them.

Outlook

Budget analyses and advocacy are key intervention points for CSOs in shaping public expenditure policy. Because of its budget advocacy activities, CBA has prepared inputs for consideration and possible inclusion in the 2006 and 2007 budgets, while exposing weak areas in Ghana's budget policies and inequities and inadequacies in the budgetary allocations and disbursements, which have compelled the government to address them.

Key Intervention Points for CSOs and Recommendations for Next Steps

Civil society groups need to be willing to not only share their views and research findings but seek audience with policymakers and lawmakers, lobby for proposed reforms, and try to ensure (acting, if necessary, in collaboration with other stakeholders) that key issues are addressed. Mass action, including demonstrations, may become necessary when policymakers and lawmakers refuse to act appropriately. Policy briefs are one way of engaging policymakers and lawmakers in decisionmaking and implementation. The CBA started writing policy briefs for parliament but could not sustain them. The SEND

Foundation has sought audience with the Ministry of Finance and Economic Planning on its tracking results. The Ghana National Education Campaign Coalition has sought audience with the Ministry of Education, Science, and Sports on its tracking of capitation grants.

It is important to strengthen CSOs so that they can engage effectively in dialogue with the state in the policymaking process. Training civil society representatives on the budget process equips them with the knowledge and skills to engage with key players in shaping public expenditure policy. Civil society groups interested in promoting transparency and accountability and in influencing the budget process must be familiar with the budget cycle so that they are able to determine the best entry points for inputs. The CBA has trained not only CSOs but also public officials in improving their skills in formulating and executing budgets and adopting the basic principles of a people-centered budgeting process, that is, transparency, participation, and accountability.

Workshops, seminars, public forums, and public lectures are essential in educating the general public to understand the policy issues and the duties and responsibilities of officeholders and service providers, as well as key issues in resource allocation, so as to demand transparency, accountability, and quality service delivery. These activities have been going on but not on a large-scale basis. The media contribute much and could be supported to further pursue this work.

CSOs must disseminate their budget and policy analyses and the findings of monitoring and tracking exercises because this is essential for achieving transparency and accountability. Thus the CBA has held press conferences and public forums on national budgets to disseminate views on the budgets. The launch of survey reports, such as Transparency International's Corruption Perception Index, the *Global Corruption Report,* the Global Corruption Barometer report produced by TI's local chapter, Ghana Integrity Initiative (GII), and the International Budget Partnership's Open Budget Index, has drawn attention to transparency gaps and corruption. The media are a very important ally in these activities and have also succeeded in compelling investigations into allegations of corruption against some public officeholders following investigative reporting. In addition to ensuring working relations with the media, CSOs must build coalitions with other NGOs, which do not work directly on transparency and accountability, to mobilize the necessary support for public expenditure policy reforms.

Information on policies, laws, and local and national budgets and research findings needs to be simplified and published in suitable form for public consumption. When possible, important findings should be translated into widely spoken local languages to promote better understanding. This is necessary for public mobilization and support for the proposed reforms and action on research findings and recommendations. For example, the constitution and the Poverty Reduction Strategy have been adapted into simplified versions for public dissemination.

The monitoring of project execution and the tracking of resource flows from central government to local authorities and communities—as well as the assessment of budget performance and service delivery—are important intervention points for shaping public expenditure policy. These activities form part of social accountability initiatives, which also help build capacities among civil society and public and private institutions through training and facilitating citizen engagement in the monitoring of pro-poor projects and programs and engagement with appropriate authorities on the findings. This can improve service delivery and create a sense of local ownership of projects and programs. There is a need not only to intensify training on social auditing capabilities but also to encourage the formation of social audit committees and to encourage ordinary citizens to ask probing questions, including questioning the lifestyles of public officeholders.

There is a need for the institutionalization of civil society engagement in the decisionmaking process. This will ensure that all public officials consult civil society in whatever decisions they plan to take and, when required, provide civil society with the relevant information for its research and advocacy activities.

Some CSOs have encountered problems getting information from some government agencies. As such, civil groups in Ghana and across the African continent have seen the need for freedom of information legislation. In Ghana in particular, they have engaged in lobbying and advocacy for the enactment of an FOI bill, which has been on the drawing board for almost ten years. Closely linked to this is advocacy for the amendment and enforcement of Ghana's assets declaration law as a tool for curbing corruption.

Civil society must not only advocate for transparency-enhancing and anti-corruption laws but should make inputs at the initial stages of the enactment process and not wait for the laws to be enacted and then criticize them. GII has initiated action to make an input into the review of the Assets Declaration Act and the Public Procurement Act. However, in most cases proposed bills are not readily available to the public during their design stages.

Interventions by Donors and External Organizations

Donors and external organizations can provide core institutional funding to CSOs that are working to promote transparency and accountability to help them pay competitive wages, offer training, and meet running costs. Often, many donors provide funding only for the costs of a specific project, assuming that the CSO is already well established and has all the needed skilled employees and equipment. Unfortunately, this is not the situation in many CSOs. Even when the CSOs are well established, increased demands on staff effort and time require more compensation and increased running costs. Monitoring and tracking activities are very expensive and require financial support from donors and external organizations. Some support is being provided, but it needs to be increased and expanded to cover more CSOs.

Secondly, donors and global civil society organizations can provide technical support to CSOs to improve their knowledge and skills on budget and policy analyses, budget tracking, and performance assessment. Furthermore, for effective advocacy, the media are a necessary ally in disseminating monitoring results and advocacy activities. Therefore, external actors can support CSOs to set up their own media operations or support existing CSO media functions. Some CSOs produce newsletters and have websites, but these need to be improved. In addition, assistance to state agencies for maintenance of information and records would be welcome, specifically computerization of recordkeeping, which would facilitate accessibility as well.

External players can insist on transparency and accountability as a requirement for their assistance. Most donors emphasize good governance as a requirement for their support but may take an unduly narrow view of what is involved in good governance. That needs to change. Donors can support monitoring groups in their demands for the recovery of lost assets, redirection of resources, termination of contracts to ensure improved quality of programs and projects, and the avoidance of waste and inefficiency in the use of public resources. If donors showed interest in these reports, given the power and influence they wield in the budget process, government would be compelled to take them more seriously.

Civil Society Strengthening in Budget Processes—A Critical Issue

Civil society action has become essential in shaping public expenditure policy, because Ghana's resource constraints require better prioritization of policies and effective budgeting, improved efficiency, and the avoidance of waste. Corruption is a major governance problem in the face of weak and ineffective powers of prosecution of corruption cases.[6] Moreover, the government has recently been receiving funds from financial markets in China and other emerging creditors, piling up debt for future generations. It is thus imperative

6. APRM (2005).

that civil society organizations be strengthened so that they can promote transparency and accountability as they grapple with financial and technical resource constraints, including lack of experienced staff and equipment.

Government officials are often reluctant to assist CSOs with the needed resources and relevant information because of mistrust and weak CSO-state relationships. The long-awaited freedom of information legislation would have enabled CSOs to compel public officials to release information when it is available (recognizing that there are genuine situations when reliable data, especially disaggregated data on programs and projects, are just not available). Many CSOs also face a major challenge in meeting the costs involved in collecting their own data. Thus most of them are compelled to rely on the available records of the Ghana Statistical Service and other agencies, including the statistics units of the relevant MDAs and the MMDAs. Strengthening CSOs to build their own databases and undertake sophisticated research is critical in the struggle for transparency and accountability.

The Future of Civil Society Engagement

Because of the improvements in democratic practices, the emergence of civil society, and the recognition by the government and donors that civil society engagement is very important, there does not appear to be any going back for the country. Some reforms have been initiated and some legislation enacted to support these reforms. Civil society will continue to support and advocate for these reforms since the problems have been in the implementation of policy initiatives and enforcement of the laws.

In the next decade, one can expect many more CSOs to emerge and join the crusade for transparency and accountability as well as anticorruption. CSO budget analyses and advocacy will no longer remain the preserve of think tanks and a few CSOs. This expansion of monitoring and advocacy activities will be enhanced by the new interest of donors and international NGOs in transparency and accountability. It likely will be enhanced further by the passage of freedom of information legislation, as pressure is brought to bear on the government from in-country and international civil society. Other CSOs may not engage in budget analysis, but they can definitely demand equitable allocations and the efficient utilization of budget resources.

One can expect to see results from the training and other programs conducted by CSOs that are aimed at raising public awareness and sensitizing public officeholders. Ordinary citizens may well become bolder in demanding transparency and accountability as well as questioning the lifestyles of officeholders. The current monitoring and tracking activities could increase as well, and civil society would be able to identify and expose leakage in resource disbursement and utilization of budget resources and thereby compel government to redress the situation. The interface meetings that are held under some of the participatory performance assessments would draw the attention of service providers since poor performance would be exposed to their supervisors, which, it is hoped, would compel action to improve performance.

GILBERT KHADIAGALA

B
Transparency and Accountability in Kenya's Budget Process

Historical Governance Context

For many years following its independence from Britain in 1963, Kenya witnessed relative political stability and economic prosperity compared with most of its East African neighbors. This was primarily attributable to the existence of fairly sturdy institutions such as the bureaucracy, a sizable middle class based in agriculture and industry, tolerance for foreign investment, and remarkable levels of ethnic, racial, and social amity. Britain also bequeathed a strong judiciary, rule of law, a vibrant press, and a multiparty parliamentary democracy that gave Kenya a solid head start in governance.

Barely five years into independence, however, under the leadership of President Jomo Kenyatta, Kenya changed course toward a one-party presidential system with the Kenya African National Union (KANU) as the de facto sole party. The transition to a one-party state also coincided with Kenyatta's increasing reliance on his ethnic group, the Kikuyu, who came increasingly to control the bureaucracy, political life, and much of the economy. Throughout the 1960s and 1970s, economic prosperity and an elaborate system of political patronage helped tame ethnic animosities. Similarly, periodic elections provided a modicum of participation, blunting the edges of Kenyatta's authoritarianism. Kenyatta encouraged foreign private investment alongside a public sector composed of state-owned enterprises. As a consequence, European and Asian capital coexisted uneasily with the regime's populist policies of Africanization that promoted African ownership of the economy. When Kenyatta died in 1978, he left a mixed record that included relatively strong economic growth (averaging about 6 percent); high population growth rates;

weak participatory institutions that largely had been overwhelmed by an authoritarian executive; and a functioning bureaucracy that was nonetheless heavily ethnically based.

President Daniel Arap Moi, from the minority Kalenjin ethnic group, succeeded Kenyatta and inaugurated a twenty-four-year-period of institutional decay, economic stagnation, ethnic polarization, and social malaise. Moi's rule coincided with new and virulent strains of disease, including the HIV/AIDS pandemic; rampant urbanization; declining foreign investment; the informalization of the economy; and the militarization of society. From the outset, Moi focused primarily on undoing the delicate ethnic balancing act that had been the hallmark of Kenyatta's governance. His attempts to play off ethnic groups against each other created political uncertainty and eroded KANU's previous role of providing a semblance of political participation. Instead, KANU became a blatant machine to reward proponents and punish opponents.[1] Under Moi, economic mismanagement, corruption, and wanton destruction of national resources became rampant. Although concerted pressures from donors and civic groups in the early 1990s forced a return to multiparty democracy, the political opening concealed the continuity of authoritarian practices that persisted for another decade. Moi adopted multiparty democracy to fend off prying donors but proceeded to subvert opposition parties by unleashing violence, sponsoring splinter parties to divide the weak opposition, and expending state resources to win the elections of 1992 and 1997. Some segments of the Moi government also mobilized ethnic militias against the opposition, paving the way for the militarization of society along ethnic and sectarian lines.[2]

Although the Moi regime focused on frustrating the democratic transition, the limited democratic space emboldened new social and political actors across ethnic and functional lines to work toward a hoped-for transition to pluralism and political competition. Civil society actors, in particular the middle class in professional organizations, farmers and trade unions, and religious organizations, carved out a strategic niche in the governance debates from the early 1990s. Similarly, donors pressed for economic reforms, including measures intended to promote a revival in professionalism in the management of public resources in a bid to counter corruption and related problems. The Moi regime only reluctantly conceded to donor involvement in monitoring economic governance, but gradually new

1. Klopp (2001); Ndegwa (1998); Holmquist and Ford (1992).
2. Kahl (1998); Khadiagala (1995).

institutions and actors coalesced around goals of transparency, accountability, and probity.[3]

President Kibaki, another Kikuyu, took power following the elections in December 2002. These elections themselves epitomized the increasing maturity of civil society organizations seeking genuine political change. The momentum for change also unleashed an interethnic alliance, the National Rainbow Coalition (NARC), composed of members of most of the large ethnic groups—Kikuyu, Luo, Luhya, and Kamba—seeking to reverse Kenya's descent into economic meltdown, political unrest, and state failure. Kibaki's landslide victory galvanized core sections of society seeking to undo the scourge of corruption, lawlessness, and profound disrespect for public institutions. Five years into the Kibaki presidency, however, despite remarkable progress on the economic front and the steady resurrection of governance institutions, there was widespread uncertainty about the depth and direction of political and economic reforms.[4] Since 2003 ethnic turbulence and the jostling for power paralyzed decisionmaking and reignited the past practices of corruption, impunity, and subversion of formal institutions by informal ones. NARC failed to live up to the long-standing promise for fundamental revisions to the independence constitution that were supposed to entrench the structures for stable governance, particularly the reduction of excessive executive powers. When the government lost a popular referendum on the constitution in November 2005, it began to resort to tactics of authoritarianism, police brutality, press censorship, and ethnic manipulation.[5]

By the time of Kenya's elections of December 2007, the picture of governance in Kenya was decidedly mixed. Democratization had opened more vistas for participation, but old patterns of ethnic polarization and patronage continued to cast a cloud over political stability. NARC's earlier triumph had symbolized the significance of coalitions for a stable political order, but extant coalitions were essentially elite machines for winning power rather than genuine avenues for political participation. Public institutions of accountability and governance had received a new impetus that had yet to be deepened, resulting in the resurgence of cronyism and corruption. Civic organizations that germinated during the authoritarian era remained vibrant, but they had suffered serious transition trauma, falling prey to ethnic identities, partisan

3. Ndegwa (1997); Holmquist and Ford (1998).
4. Steeves (2006).
5. Cottrell and Ghai (2007).

politics, and government interference. Consequently, there had been visible declines in coherent civic alertness and vigilance.[6]

Diagnosis

The budget process in Kenya takes place within the larger picture of governance and institutional change described above. Experience over the last two decades demonstrates that the quality of governance, the balance of power among branches of government, and the societal quest for inclusiveness have mattered in bids to find better approaches to the articulation and implementation of national economic priorities. But despite the desire by wider segments of society for inclusion in decisions on public expenditures, Kenya's budgetary process has continued to be dominated by highly centralized executive institutions. Although the era of one-party regimes (1963–91) deepened executive dominance over budgets, the onset of multiparty politics (1991–present) has not fundamentally altered this picture. New constituencies and institutions have proliferated to agitate against the budgetary status quo, but they have yet to find a coherent voice and institutional anchor. In the absence of constitutional changes that perceptibly shift the relationship between the presidency and parliament and inject an element of governmental accountability to society, the budget process will remain hostage to executive hegemony, weak parliamentary oversight, and societal apathy toward budget questions.

Since the late 1980s, donor-driven budget reforms have attempted to streamline the process, enhance fiscal discipline, improve the efficiency of resource allocation, and undercut the informal structures of power that have fueled corruption. The first generation of budget reforms in the 1980s entailed measures to link annual budgets to development plans, but it was not until 2000 that the government introduced the World Bank's medium-term expenditure framework (MTEF) as the core platform for budget reforms. The MTEF is designed to restore credibility to the budget process by defining a three-year macroeconomic framework that makes it possible to establish national priorities within a realistic resource framework.[7] Although informal

---

6. This appendix was originally prepared before the Kenyan elections of December 2007. The elections led to a contested outcome, in which President Kibaki claimed victory over the protests of opposition parties, while many independent observers raised questions about the conduct of the vote count. Following several weeks of political violence, largely along ethnic lines, Kibaki and his leading opponent, Raila Odinga, agreed on a power-sharing coalition in which Kibaki continued as president while Odinga became prime minister. (*Editor*).

7. Kiringai and West (2002); Khasiani and Makau (2004, pp. 21–34); Oyugi (2005); Masya and Njiraini (2003).

institutions of power that have been the hallmarks of the patronage system still continue to characterize decisionmaking on the budget, one of the primary objectives of the MTEF is to make the budget process more transparent through inclusion of multiple actors.

Principal Actors

A key objective of MTEF was to establish better links between planning and budgeting: roles that had been divided between, respectively, the Ministry of Planning and National Development and the Ministry of Finance. These two agencies continue to be the principal actors in the budgetary process. As part of the MTEF, new technical institutions were established under the overall direction of the Ministry of Finance to inject a stronger dose of accountability and transparency in budget formulation and implementation. Some of these institutions include the following:

—*MTEF Secretariat*: Established in the Ministries of Finance and Planning and National Development, the secretariat coordinates and directs the implementation of MTEF on a full-time basis. It is also in charge of capacity building for key participants in the budget process.

—*Macroeconomic working group (MWG)*: Chaired by the director of planning in the Ministry of Planning and National Development, the MWG's members are drawn from the relevant departments in the Ministries of Finance and Planning and National Development, the Kenya Institute for Public Policy and Research Analysis, the Kenya Revenue Authority, and the Central Bank of Kenya. It may also co-opt other specialized institutions when the need arises. The MWG is responsible for preparing consistent forecasts for economic development and growth, sets the broad parameters under which budgetary priorities are fashioned, prepares estimates of expected revenues and the financing strategy for public expenditures, and together with the sector working groups proposes sectoral resource ceilings.

—*Sectoral working groups (SWGs)*: There are eight sectoral working groups: public administration, public safety and law and order, physical infrastructure, health, agriculture and rural development, education, general economic services, and national security. Working closely with line ministries, the SWGs are responsible for developing sectoral policies and objectives, evaluating ministry and department budget submissions, and ensuring that the activities and outcomes conform to national objectives. Each sector has a core secretariat based at the Ministry of Planning and National Development, which incorporates ministries and other stakeholders when required.

—*Budget Steering Committee*: Established in the Ministry of Finance, the committee is composed of heads of Departments of Budget, Economic

Affairs, Debt Management, External Resources, Accountant General, Pensions, Government Information Technology Services, and the Macroeconomic Department of the Ministry of Planning and National Development. It considers budget proposals and monitors developments that may arise in the course of implementation of the budget.

—*Office of the Controller and Auditor General (CAG)*: As one of the primary watchdog agencies over public expenditures, the CAG publishes annual reports that catalogue incidents of financial malpractice and scandals ranging from fraudulent evasion of tax, wastage of public funds, and corruption, particularly in procurement processes. The reports have been an essential source of information for civil society actors to raise issues about the allocation of public resources. In turn, groups at the grass roots have been able to effectively engage the government on its acts and omissions with regard to public finances. For instance, after the much-publicized Anglo Leasing contracts scandal, which involved fraudulent procurement of security-related services, the CAG made several recommendations that were used by civil society to engage parliament in all phases of the security components of the budget, including procurement, priority setting, and oversight.[8]

—*The National Economic and Social Council (NESC)*: Formed in January 2005 to foster dialogue between the government and the private sector and to advise the president on economic priorities, the NESC is chaired by the president and mostly is made up of leading corporate figures in Kenya. It was instrumental in adopting Vision 2030, a development blueprint that seeks to jump-start Kenya into the status of a newly industrializing country.

Given Kenya's bureaucratic culture of hierarchy and insularity, most of these institutions are striving to introduce more transparency by promoting better coordination and dialogue about planning and budget priorities across government institutions. Proponents of these reforms have contended that, pending constitutional changes, the new institutions that are focused on the budget are starting incrementally to reduce executive supremacy over the budget through the infusion of elements of transparency and accountability.[9] Most assessments of the MTEF reforms recognize that, while the innovations adopted to date represent improvements, the objectives of fiscal discipline and allocation efficiency are long-term ones and will require support at the political level. In the short-to-medium terms, although the MTEF approach

8. See the *Daily Nation*, March 31, 2006.

9. Institute of Economic Affairs (2003); Transparency International (2004), see especially chapter 24.

has not resolved all problems pertaining to the management of public resources, it has contributed to enhancing the clarity of roles and responsibilities of actors in the budgetary process.[10]

Role of Parliament

The Kenyan constitution recognizes the role of parliament in the budget process, nominally delineated in terms of authorization, oversight, and supervision. In reality, however, the legislature has had limited authority to hold the executive accountable for sound financial management, operating for the most part under the whims of the executive.[11]

With the onset of competitive politics, parliament has ridden on the wave of transparency and accountability to recapture some of the space afforded by the constitution. As part of these efforts, parliament passed a Parliamentary Service Commission Act in 1999 to delink itself from the executive.[12] Through the parliamentary Public Accounts Committee (PAC) and the Public Investment Committee (PIC), parliament has tried to exert a measure of legislative oversight. These committees are empowered by the constitution to seek information relating to public expenditure in public institutions in which the government has at least a 51 percent equity share.

In a landmark piece of legislation passed by parliament in October 2005, members of parliament proposed changes in the budget-making process to give themselves the power to vet the government's spending proposals in the budget through a new committee, the Fiscal Analysis and Appropriations Committee. With a membership of fourteen appointed to sit on the committee for a five-year term, the committee is supposed to guarantee more continuity in parliamentary oversight. Unlike the PAC and PIC, which perform postexpenditure audits, the new committee is supposed to review and make proposals to the Ministry of Finance before the budget is presented to parliament. To assist the committee and parliament's overall ability to manage public finance, the Parliamentary Service Commission also established a Budget Secretariat manned by professional officers.

Parliament also created new institutions to provide members of parliament (MPs) with a more direct say in public spending at the grassroots level, including the Constituency Development Fund (CDF) and the Bursary Fund.

10. Institute of Economic Affairs (2004); Kenya Institute for Public Policy Research and Analysis (2004); Hanmer and others (2003).

11. Parliamentary Center (2002).

12. Barkan (2004).

In the 2005 financial year, the government set aside 5.6 billion shillings (about US$90 million) for the CDF, with each constituency receiving an average of 24 million shillings to finance projects in the education, health, and water sectors. The Bursary Fund, meanwhile, is money allotted to MPs to provide education subsidies to individuals deemed to be in need.[13]

As part of parliamentary bids to reverse years of perfunctory performance by the legislature in economic decisionmaking, there have been efforts to enhance legislative training and capacity building. Donors have invested in parliamentary committees to enable MPs to become meaningful participants in the budget process. Similarly, parliament has agitated for changes that would make the Controller and Auditor General's Office more accountable to its committees rather than to the executive. Parliamentary activism has also focused on efforts to establish stronger anticorruption bodies, including the Economic Crimes Bill, and the establishment of the Kenya Anti-Corruption Commission and the Anti-Corruption Campaign Commission.

Role of Civil Society Organizations

The inclusion of nonstate actors, in particular civil society advocates, in budget formulation is one of the outcomes of political and economic liberalization. Reforms have fostered the inclusion of multifaceted voices in the budget process, with the goal of diminishing the authoritarianism that has long dominated economic decisionmaking. The legal framework for the budget process has no provisions for participation by civil society and the public at large, but the incorporation of these actors resulted from the diverse pressures for pluralism and participatory governance. Toward this end, MTEF fostered engagement between civil society and government in the budget process, underscoring the need for more robust public participation in the management of public finances and resources. Greater participation could be justified by the fact that the bulk of the budget process has typically been shrouded in mystery, with bureaucrats playing a disproportionate role in all crucial resource allocation decisions. The mechanisms for public engagement involve attendance by interested members of the public at budget hearing sessions to express their views on spending priorities.

13. While the CDF has been presented by some as an innovative link between parliament and citizens on budgetary and resource allocation issues, the management of the fund has come under criticism in many constituencies, as MPs have been accused of handpicking relatives and political allies on CDF committees. In Transparency International's *The Kenya Bribery Index 2007* report, the CDF was ranked eighth on the list of ten most corrupt institutions.

To deepen public participation in budget issues, the consultative process for the 2001–04 Poverty Reduction Strategy Paper (PRSP) involved a coalition of nonstate actors that constituted one of the pillars of the National Stakeholders (government, parliament, NGOs, and the private sector). Overall, the PRSP process is a critical experiment in fostering open dialogue between the government and civil society across the entire domain of economic decisionmaking, inaugurating partnerships that did not exist before. By creating a national consultative framework, the PRSP has also forced government to be more open about its roles, and thus it slowly started to force more effective dissemination of information about the budget.[14]

The Media

The media regained their stature and standing as a watchdog in the era of political liberalization. In recent years, Kenya's vibrant press has been indispensable in nurturing an informed citizenry. Perhaps more than parliament and nonstate actors, the press has become an accountability police, keeping the government on its toes and being a creative irritant to the leadership. In circumstances when information has not been readily available to the public, the media have contributed to broadening transparency and sparking debates on vital economic issues, including the budget. Despite constitutional restrictions, media vibrancy has resulted from the widening political space, in contrast to earlier years when censorship and self-censorship predominated. It was partly in recognition of this growing role that the government recently tried to reintroduce coercive media legislation when parliament passed the Media Bill of 2007, which would have forced the media to reveal their sources. After a widespread outcry by the local media (and donor agencies), the government rescinded the media law.

Private Sector

Various private sector bodies have lobbied the government on budget issues, including the Kenya Private Sector Alliance, an umbrella body representing more than 200 sectors and organizations, and the Kenya Association of Manufacturers. Given the centrality of the private sector since independence, the government often listens to these organizations, particularly on issues of investment in public goods and the adoption of investor-friendly policies, all of which have budgetary implications. Key members of the private sector

14. Hanmer and others (2003); Freeman, Ellis, and Allison (2004); Kiringai and Manda (2002).

have also served on government economic committees and task forces, reflecting an increasing drive to promote private-public partnerships.

Signals and Actions in the Budget Process

In the Kenyan context where the executive, acting in large part through budget bureaucrats in core ministries, exerts disproportionate leverage over the budget, questions of relative power hinge on the ability of institutions such as parliament, civil society, the private sector, and the media to seize opportunities and exploit weaknesses in the power structures to effect changes in budget priorities. Although these opportunities have accrued from gradual expansion of the space for democracy, mass agitation for clean government, and societal vigilance, their successful exploitation is dependent, for the most part, on the organizational abilities and creativity of the institutions concerned to push the institutional envelope. Moreover, since the budget cycle remains hierarchical and top-down, the ability of representative institutions and nonstate actors to prevail will depend on their ability to leverage entry points, wherever they exist within the budget cycle.

Although recent government pronouncements claim that the budget is "the Government's contract with the nation," Kenya's annual budget cycle is not in fact very participatory. The cycle starts in October of each year. Under the MTEF process, the Ministry of Finance sets ceilings for all eight sectors on a three-year basis. During sessions of the sectoral working groups, different ministries, with limited input from outside groups, establish and harmonize sector priorities with national priorities. The public is only afforded a passing opportunity through the annual prebudget hearings, which have been encouraged to include the voice of the citizens in budget drafting. But there is little evidence that any of the views expressed in these sector hearings have actually been adopted in the final financial estimates. As one critic has contended, "The budget hearings are yet to evolve into a forum that can promote robust discussions and debate, where government priorities can be subjected to thorough scrutiny and where civil servants can be made accountable on their spending decisions."

Past efforts to solicit memoranda from experts on budget proposals have not broadened participation, particularly from grassroots organizations. Consequently, while the incorporation of civil society actors in budget reforms has established participatory parameters, there are still considerable obstacles to achieving significant civil society influence over budget outcomes. The organizational abilities of these actors leave a lot to be desired. In addition, civil society actors often do not speak with one voice, because they represent diverse constituencies and have varying levels of competencies. Besides, the technical nature of the budget process, in addition to the inadequate information available to civil society actors, limits their capacity to guarantee the transparency of the budget.[15]

Like civil society organizations, parliament intervenes in the budgetary process at a time when most of the priorities already have been established through the sectoral working groups and the preliminary budget estimates have been presented to parliament (in June). In their oversight roles, members of parliament debate and pass the allocations for individual ministries between June and October. Potentially, MPs can change priorities and estimates during this process. But there are two impediments to parliamentary efficacy in the budget process. First, the constitution has a provision called the guillotine, whereby the government can lump the budgets of most ministries in one basket and force a parliamentary vote on them without debate and scrutiny. Devices to manage the time allowed for debate are used in many other legislatures, but the guillotine as actually operated in Kenya has allowed the executive to pass billions of shillings for questionable projects without scrutiny by MPs.

Second, the record of Kenyan MPs reveals that budget issues are often far from the top of their priorities, as evidenced by the persistent lack of a parliamentary quorum during the discussion and passage of budget bills. Although some of the reforms initiated since 2005 are intended to provide better parliamentary oversight in the key phases of the budget cycle, the performance of Kenya's parliament is problematic. In 2005, parliament failed to seize opportunities, for instance, when it voted on key ministerial budget appropriations without a quorum. Despite legislative training, parliament has hardly improved from the days when it was a mere rubber stamp for the executive. More worrisome for effective representation has been the anarchic nature of political party aggregation in Kenya. The efficacy of parliament in the multiparty era depends on stable national parties with individuals who have a smattering of enduring principles. The inchoate state of political parties reflects the fraying of coalition politics and the opportunism that colors political parties. Since 2003, instability in political parties has affected the quality of representation, adding a complex layer of uncertainty to parliamentary decisionmaking, particularly as it has sometimes been difficult to reach agreements on membership of parliamentary budget committees, including budget committees.

15. CLARION (2003); African Development Bank (2001).

In addition to limited representative and public engagement in budget formulation, nonstate actors are not involved in decisions during the budget *implementation* phase.[16] The executive commands considerable constitutional leeway over how budget resources are actually spent, primarily through the handling of implementation, extra-budgetary appropriations, auditing, and monitoring. Despite campaigns to allow public participation in implementation decisions, the government has yet to agree to public involvement in systems to monitor actual government expenditures.

Outlook

In the absence of changes in the constitutional framework to delineate roles and responsibilities in ways that would be better suited to an era of multiparty politics, there is a need to step up capacity building interventions tailored at single institutional actors and at multiple actors across government, parliament, and nonstate sectors. Donors such as DfID and USAID, for instance, have started only in recent years to take parliamentary training programs on budget-related issues more seriously. Parliamentarians are still hamstrung by structural and attitudinal obstacles, as noted earlier, and in addition, the task of building the competence of parliamentary committees in economic affairs has barely began. As multiparty structures take root and assuming that parliament's role in resource allocation grows, interventions that boost the technical skills of parliamentarians may be necessary. Similarly, there are various programs to raise the capacity of the media to perform their watchdog role in general terms, but few programs that directly target media capacity specifically in budget and planning questions. The dearth of journalists knowledgeable in economic issues has long dogged Kenya, despite its vibrant media. It may be prudent to build better economic understanding within the media, with a view to boosting journalists' ability to articulate and disseminate budget information.

As amorphous as they are, civil society actors perform a crucial advocacy role in economic issues, but like the media, they lack deep knowledge of the fundamental questions. The absence of a meaningful NGO voice on budget issues stems in part from the fact that advocacy groups typically have weak expertise on the technical and functional questions entailed in budgetary affairs. There is, however, an emerging trend in Kenya in which interventions are structured around deepening the capacity of professional associations

16. Cheru (2006); IPAR (2004).

whose role in specific functional areas may be more germane than that of the traditional, multipurpose NGOs. An example would be efforts to build a coalition of technical NGOs with knowledge about procurement issues so that they become key actors in procurement reforms. In future, interventions could usefully be geared toward increasing existing knowledge in core budget reform areas within business associations, university departments, and competent NGOs. Furthermore, the civil society coalitions stimulated by the PRSP consultative process could be drawn upon for capacity building and training, because they have winnowed out many civil society actors and institutions that are less relevant for these types of issues.

Perennial contests over the budget among a wide array of actors depend on the relative strength of these actors in the political domain. Budget contests mirror the sturdiness of governance institutions, particularly the ways that the executive negotiates its spending and taxation priorities with representative institutions and the wider citizenry but also how oversight agencies guarantee sound implementation of budget compromises. In Kenya, the opening of budget processes to societal input is a relatively recent phenomenon, the outcome of a tentative reform dynamic driven largely by widespread pressures for political and economic change. Given the previous gulf between the citizens and government on forging national priorities, the baby steps unleashed by the reforms constitute important beginnings in institutional change. The legacy of tight executive control of the budget abounds, but reforms have ushered in some changes that have sought incrementally to check budgetary indiscipline, as well as government waste, neglect, and misallocation of resources. Moreover, as the reforms have propelled islands of efficiency and probity, they have contributed to building some measure of transparency and accountability into the national budgetary process.

Even if constitutional reforms to underpin a more transparent and participatory budget process remain stalemated, the most promising avenue for upholding the reforms is to be found in the constituencies created or empowered by the changes of the 1990s. These changes expanded the dialogue on social and economic policies by incorporating multiple actors that remain visible on the socioeconomic horizon. In addition, some oversight bodies created to meet donor pressures have acquired lives of their own, which could potentially help underwrite future reforms. Where parliament as the central representative institution is in disarray and where the legacy of executive dominance and opaqueness prevails, an articulate and engaged citizenry is the linchpin of reforms. Although society at large lacks the capacity to use and demand information for effective transparency and accountability, years of civic education have started to bear fruit, nurturing diverse constituencies with profound stakes in good government.

Since the June 2006 budget, Kenya has stated the intention of weaning itself from donor financing. If this truly were to happen, it potentially could remove an important source of external leverage for reforms. But the government's determination to boost local revenues by broadening the bracket of taxpayers could itself represent an ideal avenue for building genuine stakeholders with an enduring interest in public expenditure and the allocation of tax revenues. Greater awareness on the part of the taxpaying public could help create permanent bulwarks against abuse of public resources and strengthen demands for clean institutions. There are numerous actors and institutions brought into play by the past reforms that retain sufficient credibility to sustain a new generation of reforms around the budget process and beyond. How hospitable the national political environment will be in coming years to a further deepening of civic involvement of these kinds remains to be seen.

References

African Development Bank. 2001. "Governance in Africa: The Role for Information and Communication Technologies." Economic Research Paper 65. Abidjan. (N.B., published in 2001 but indexed at AfDB website under 2004).

Barkan, Joel. 2004. "Kenya after Moi." *Foreign Affairs* 83, no. 1: 87–100.

Cheru, Fantu. 2006. "Building and Supporting PRSPs in Africa. What Has Worked Well So Far? What Needs Changing?" *Third World Quarterly* 27, no. 2: 355–76.

CLARION. 2003. Public Finance Management in Kenya: A Review of the Draft Bill of the Constitution of Kenya Commission. Nairobi: Center for Law and Research International (CLARION).

Cottrell, Jill, and Yash Ghai. 2007. "Constitution Making and Democratization in Kenya (2000–2005)." *Democratization* 14, no. 1: 1–25.

Freeman, H., F. Ellis, and E. Allison. 2004. "Livelihoods and Rural Poverty Reduction in Kenya." *Development Policy Review* 22, no. 2: 147–71.

Hanmer, Lucian, and others. 2003. "Kenya." *Development Policy Review* 21 (March): 179–96.

Holmquist, Frank, and Michael Ford. 1992. "Kenya: Slouching toward Democracy." *Africa Today* 39, no. 3: 97–111.

———. 1998. "Kenyan Politics: Toward a Second Transition?" *Africa Today* 45, no. 2: 227–58.

Institute of Economic Affairs. 2003. *Budget Transparency: Kenya Perspective.* Research Paper 4. Nairobi: IEA.

———. 2004. *2003 Annual Report.* Nairobi: IEA.

IPAR. 2004. *District Focus for Rural Development in Kenya: Its Limitation as a Decentralization and Participatory Planning Strategy and Prospects for the Future. Policy Brief* 10, no. 9. Nairobi: Institute of Policy Analysis and Research.

Kahl, Colin H. 1998. "Population Growth, Environmental Degradation, and State-Sponsored Violence: The Case of Kenya, 1991–93." *International Security* 23, no. 2: 80–119.

Kenya Institute for Public Policy Research and Analysis. 2004. "Budget Mechanisms and Public Expenditure Tracking in Kenya." Discussion Paper 37. Nairobi.

Khadiagala, Gilbert. 1995. "Kenya: Intractable Authoritarianism." *SAIS Review* 14, no. 2: 53–73.

Khasiani, Kubia, and Phyllis Makau. 2004. "Kenya: Integrating Expenditure towards Policy Priorities." In *Budget Reform Seminar: Country Case Studies.* Pretoria, South Africa: Collaborative Africa Budget Reform Initiative.

Kiringai, Jane, and Damiano Kulunda Manda. 2002. "The PRSP Process in Kenya." Paper presented at the second meeting of the African Learning Group on the Poverty Reduction Strategy. Brussels, November, 18–21, 2002.

Kiringai, Jane, and G. West. 2002. "Budget Reforms and the Medium Term Expenditure Framework in Kenya." Working Paper 7. Nairobi: Kenya Institute for Public Policy Research and Analysis.

Klopp, Jacqueline M. 2001. "'Ethnic Clashes' and Winning Elections: The Case of Kenya's Electoral Despotism." *Canadian Journal of African Studies* 35, no. 2: 473–517.

Masya, Japhet K., and Peter Njiraini. 2003. "Budgetary Process in Kenya: Enhancement of Its Public Accountability." Discussion Paper 040/2003. Nairobi: Institute of Policy Analysis and Research.

Ndegwa, Stephen N. 1997. "Citizenship and Ethnicity: An Examination of Two Transition Moments in Kenyan Politics." *American Political Science Review* 91, no. 3: 599–616.

———. 1998. "The Incomplete Transition: The Constitutional and Electoral Context in Kenya." *Africa Today* 42, no. 2: 193–211.

Oyugi, Lineth N. 2005. "The Budgetary Process and Economic Governance in Kenya." Working Paper 98. Windhoek, Namibia: Namibian Economic Policy Research Network.

Parliamentary Center. 2002. *Parliamentary Accountability and Good Governance: A Parliamentarian's Handbook.* Ottawa: Parliamentary Center and the World Bank Institute.

Steeves, Jeffrey. 2006. "Presidential Succession in Kenya: The Transition from Moi to Kibaki." *Commonwealth & Comparative Politics* 44, no. 2: 211–33.

Transparency International. 2004. *Global Corruption Report 2004.* Cambridge University Press.

Transparency International-Kenya. 2007. *The Kenya Bribery Index 2007.* Nairobi.

CECILIA ZAVALLOS

C

Transparency and Accountability
in Peru's Budget Process

Historical Governance Context

During the 1990s, Peru achieved economic stabilization and managed to defeat terrorism, which had been a major problem throughout the 1980s. Alberto Fujimori's administration imposed severe adjustment policies to halt hyperinflation and reverse the fiscal deficits inherited from his predecessors. Fujimori's economic policies involved opening up the Peruvian economy, privatizing state-owned enterprises, reaching fiscal equilibrium, and gaining control of the external debt. However, Fujimori's authoritarian model left little scope for genuine citizen participation in government, and it created conditions for corruption to thrive.

After an electoral fraud scandal in 2000, Fujimori went into exile, and a transitional government was installed under Valentin Paniagua. The transitional administration was to begin the work of addressing a number of long-standing problems that, in many cases, predated Fujimori's term of office. These problems included excessive centralization of power, restricted social participation in public policy issues, and high levels of corruption in the government. These three main problems have been addressed since Fujimori's departure through, respectively, a process of decentralization, the development of space for dialogue and consultation with civil society, and improvements in transparency and access to information.

The decentralization process in Peru started in November 2001, when discussions began on changes in the relevant chapter of the constitution. In 2002 the constitution was modified, and the decentralization law, the organic law for municipalities, and the organic law for regional governments were published. Through this decentralization process, which is still under way, public administration responsibilities and the budget to accomplish them were supposed to be transferred to the regional and local governments by the end of 2007. Instruments such as Regional and Local Coordination Councils, a participatory budget process, and incentives for participation have been created to promote the success of this process. Since 2000, financial transfers to regional and local governments have increased more than 300 percent, largely underpinned by stronger public revenues from the mining sector. These transfers have been included in the official national budget since 2003. Despite the efforts that have been made with the decentralization process, however, there are still serious problems of weak capacity at the regional and local levels.

Regarding civil society participation and dialogue with the state, Fujimori's term as president witnessed an absence of genuine participation, with civil society groups merely included as executing agencies for some social programs. The 1993 constitution had established certain participatory mechanisms, but it was only in September 2001 that the Peruvian Congress recognized the 1994 Citizen Participation Law. This law constitutes the first big step to promote civil society participation. The other two major national initiatives involving civil society participation were, first, the National Accord, which was established in 2002 and involves seven political parties, seven civil society organizations, and the government, and, second, the establishment of the Coordinating Committee for Poverty Alleviation.

In 2002, after a year of joint efforts by political parties, civil society organizations, the media, and the transitional government, the congress approved the Law on Transparency and Access to Information. This law established the obligation for public entities to have web pages and to provide information regarding their budgets, procurement, investment projects, and so on. The transparency law also required each public institution to appoint a webmaster and to name an official to be explicitly responsible for updating the information provided. The law has not yet been applied fully by all government institutions; many, however, have started implementation, and civil society is monitoring progress toward full compliance.

In conclusion, there have been great advances in terms of macroeconomic stability, transparency, and civil society participation in Peru during the past decade. Nevertheless, further progress is needed with processes like capacity building in the public and private sectors, and decentralization to accomplish economic growth, poverty reduction, and the satisfaction of basic infrastructure needs at local and regional levels.

Diagnosis

The Peruvian budgetary process has five different steps from programming to evaluation and auditing. Each of these steps has several actors involved. It is also relevant to mention that, over the last few years, this process has undergone several changes in order to include civil society in programming and monitoring the national budget. To present the main actors of the budgetary process, it is important to explain these changes.

Principal Actors

The first change is the participatory budget process, which started with a pilot initiative in 2002. Through this process, civil society is included in the decisionmaking for programming the budget. This process includes capacity building through workshops and the development of a coordination plan. After the participatory budget process takes place, the results are passed to the executive so that they are included in the final proposal that is presented to the legislature. This process takes place at regional and local governments.

The second change is the Transparency and Access to Information Law. This makes it possible, through its requirements on disclosure of information by public institutions, for civil society to monitor the execution of the national budget. The law requires public institutions to publish the following information on their web pages:

—The institution's budget
—Public investment projects
—Information on the institution's employees
—Procurement
—Performance indicators

In particular, the Ministry of Economy and Finance has the obligation to publish consolidated information on public income, expenditures, debt, investment projects, and performance indicators. As a result of the Transparency and Access to Information Law, all public institutions must have a web page. The Ministry of Economy and Finance, in particular, implemented a transparency website where citizens can monitor public financial information, procurement, and transfers to local and regional governments, among other useful information. To date, the scope of these data are at the national and regional levels; there are some local governments that already comply with submitting the relevant information, but it is not yet publicly available.

The main actors that participate throughout the whole budget process are the National Directorate for Public Budget (DNPP), and each public institution through different offices. There are other actors such as the congress or the National Audit Agency (*Contraloria*) that intervene in one or two of the steps.

Main Steps and Actors in the Peruvian Budget Process

Programming. The DNPP is in charge of estimating the fiscal incomes and assigning each public institution a proportion of this income. The heads of public institutions are in charge of updating and approving the institutional objectives that are the basic instrument for preparing the institutional budgets. A priority list is established that is based on the objectives. Different units such as the budget office, the execution units, and the technical offices of each public institution provide technical assistance during this process. At the end of the process, a programming and formulation committee is formed in each institution.

Formulation. During this stage, each public institution has to define the structure of its budget by programs; establish priorities regarding the institutional objectives that were approved during the programming stage; and assign expenditures, amounts of money to be committed, and sources of financing. This information is sent to the DNPP for its consolidation in the proposal for the Annual Public Sector Budget Law.

Approval. The proposal for the Public Sector's Budget Law and the Indebtedness and Financial Equilibrium Law is required to be presented by the executive to congress by the last day of August each year. The members of the executive, represented by the president of the Council of Ministers, the minister of economy and finance, and the rest of the cabinet, are expected to defend their budgets before the congress during the process of approval, which takes about three months, until November 30. In the event that the congress fails to approve the budget, the executive can adopt a budget by legislative decree.

Execution. During the execution of the budget, each public institution is in charge of the budget that was previously allocated to it. The DNPP is in charge of the overall management of this stage, which it does through specific norms for budget execution for each level of government, that are published at the beginning of the fiscal year.

Evaluation and Auditing. For the evaluation of the public budget, the DNPP is in charge of establishing the guidelines for each public institution to start delivering information on budget execution. The institutions in charge of the evaluation are the congress, especially through the budget and general account committees, and the Peruvian audit institution, Contraloria, that receives this evaluation document.

Signals and Actions in the Budget Process

Peru's budget process exhibits a number of crucial weaknesses. One feature is that the annual assignment of a budget to each institution is basically an inertial process, that is, what the institution received last year pretty much will be what it receives the next one. There is an ongoing process that is supposed to reform the approach to budget preparation, so that allocations would be based more on results and performance indicators. However, this process is still only at an early stage. Issues regarding the establishment of goals and objectives will need to be tackled to make progress with the proposed change from an inertial to a performance-based budget.

A second striking feature of Peruvian budgets is the low share of investment: just 18 percent of all expenditures were allocated to investment projects according to the 2007 annual budget, despite Peru's huge deficit in infrastructure.

Regarding the execution stage of the public budget, there are critical problems in terms of prioritizing projects, public procurement, and developing feasibility studies for investment projects. A project or acquisition can be included in an institution's budget during the formulation stage, but there are cumbersome procedures that must be followed before the project can start or the goods or services can be purchased.

Finally, in terms of the evaluation stage, there is no process that allows assigning next year's budget according to the performance achieved by the institution in the previous year. These indicators need to be developed so that future budgets can be based on results and performance as officially intended.

Regarding auditing and transparency issues, there has been a great advance since 2002 in terms of the obligation that every public institution has to publish certain information. Nevertheless, there is still a long way to go to change the remaining culture of secrecy that sets a gap between the transparency law and actual practices—including the need for information to be available in forms that can not only be understood by public servants but also be user friendly for civil society in general.

In conclusion, even though the actors involved in the budget process have defined roles in all stages, there are important weaknesses throughout the process such as goal definition, project prioritizing, and execution and also in terms of evaluation and transparency. These problems involve all public institutions and are deeper at the regional and local levels of government, where there has been an enormous increase in public resources but a critical lack of institutional capacity. The role of civil society in the improvement of spending capacity, prioritizing, and monitoring is increasingly important in Peru.

Since about 2002, civil society organizations have helped improve public management, citizenship, transparency, and access to public information, among other topics.

Outlook

The concept of social accountability is relatively new in Peru but, since about 2002, it has grown in terms of the number of civil society organizations, their initiatives, and the scope of impact of these initiatives. This growth is a consequence of the period of corruption and secrecy that ended in 2000. Social accountability seeks to improve the quality of governance, improve the effectiveness of public policies and orient them better to citizens' demands, and empower citizens through different mechanisms.

Social Accountability in the Budget Process

The role of civil society organizations in Peru in the budget process involves several initiatives. The impact of these initiatives is often achieved through recognizing best practices or putting moral pressure on institutions that do not comply with the requirements of the Law on Transparency and Access to Information.

The participatory budget is an initiative that points in the direction of citizens' having direct impact on the budget process. This process has been successful in certain districts, but capacity building is a key element for getting people involved and trained on how to prioritize projects and monitor public spending.

Several CSOs undertake independent analyses of the budget process, with various different perspectives or focuses. The following are some examples of interventions.

Monitoring transfers to regional and local governments. This initiative seeks to inform citizens of the transfers from the central government to the local and regional governments each year. This project involved capacity building to train journalists on the formulas for the distribution of these transfers and the amounts of money that districts, provinces, and regions have received since 2000.

Monitoring investment project execution. This initiative is undertaken by *Foncodes,* a public institution that has worked to organize communities to monitor the execution of investment projects.

Monitoring social programs. The Coordinating Committee for Poverty Alleviation promotes capacity building for citizens to supervise the execution of social programs that seek to fight poverty.

Transparency in local governments. The Peruvian Press Council monitors compliance with the Law of Transparency and Access to Information as it applies to disclosure of financial information at the local level.

There are significant additional interventions that focus, among other topics, on public procurement and public expenditure on health and education. These interventions also have different ways of reaching citizens that go from publishing reports to organizing workshops with citizens, media, or authorities to build on their capacity to monitor, communicate, or assign and execute resources.

Social accountability in Peru has accomplished several changes in legislation and enforcement of existing legislation regarding transparency and access to information. At the national level, different public information systems have been created or improved to display public information (such as public institution websites, the integrated financial administration system, or mechanisms for demand-driven access to information). These initiatives have also managed to have a positive impact on sections of the public that are now more aware of the benefits of transparency and access to information for improving public management. Additionally, in terms of methodology, there are new mechanisms developed by CSOs to provide for monitoring and evaluating by civil society, promoting participation of informed citizens, and establishing cooperative alliances between the government and civil society. There are also publications for capacity building and the analysis of public administration.

Among the challenges for the coming years, CSOs should be pursuing the establishment of permanent mechanisms in public administration that incorporate social accountability mechanisms, the improvement of their communications mechanisms in terms of the authorities and civil society, and the development of objective indicators to help measure the impact of their initiatives.

References

Ciudadanos al Día (CAD). "Institutional Analysis of Transparency in the Peruvian Budget Process." Unpublished. Lima.

———. 2007. "Taking Stock and Analyzing Social Accountability Approaches and Mechanisms in Ecuador and Peru." Final Report. Lima.

Law 27806 on Transparency and Access to Information.

Law 28056 on the Participatory Budget.

Law 28927 on the Public Sector's Budget for 2007.

Shack, Nelson. 2006. "Budgeting in Peru." Santiago: Latin America and the Caribbean Institute for Economic and Social Planning (ILPES).

JUAN PARDINAS

D

Transparency and Accountability in Mexico's Budget Process

Historical Governance Context

In the last decades of the twentieth century, Mexico experienced two parallel transformations of its political system:

—The transition from a presidency that operated essentially above and beyond constitutional limits to a presidency that operates within the constitution, which involved a shift from an executive with unwritten and overarching powers to a presidency bound by written laws and the institutions in charge of enforcing them

—The evolution from a quasi-single-party system, where the president and his party (which for many decades meant the *Partido Revolucionario Institucional*, or PRI) had almost absolute control over election results, into a competitive, multiparty system with legitimate electoral institutions

In striking contrast to other democratic transitions elsewhere in Latin America or in Eastern Europe, Mexico's path to democracy did not fracture its political institutions. There was no sudden collapse of the previous regime, nor was there a collective demand for a new constitutional framework. Moreover, the legal basis of presidentialism was never challenged by any serious propositions for alternative models, such as parliamentarianism.[1] The main criticisms of the previous regime were the unwritten powers of the president and the lack of credibility of the electoral system. The proposition advanced by the critics was simple: a president bound by law and institutions, plus fair and free suffrage, would equal democracy. The constitutional scaffolding from

---

1. Lujambio (1995, pp. 11–12).

the *ancien régime* could, to a large degree, be adapted to accommodate the architecture of the new era.

For most of the twentieth century, the discretionary powers of the president had formed the basis of political stability. The challenge of Mexico's new plural political system was to create a foundation for stability without those discretionary powers. Political stability now had to be based on rules accepted by all political actors, and the institutions charged with enforcing these rules needed the collective consent (or at least acquiescence) of diverse political interests. These new institutions shared a common source of legitimacy that included political autonomy from the presidential sphere of influence.

During the 1990s, Mexico embarked on an intensive process of institutional reform in several arenas of public life. Regarding the economy, in 1993–94 the president granted the right to the Central Bank to set interest rates, the Mexican currency was allowed to float freely, and the executive lost the capability to influence the exchange rate. In 1994 the Mexican Supreme Court was restructured under the premise of gaining independence from political pressures coming from the president's office.[2]

Most of the subplots of the transition to a constitutional presidency required major reforms in secondary legislation and several constitutional changes. In the electoral arena, in 1996 the institution in charge of organizing elections (*Instituto Federal Electoral*) and the electoral courts gained political independence from the executive. At the state level, most local conflicts came to be resolved through institutional channels instead of by the ouster of governors by presidential initiative.

Diagnosis

One of the key sources of presidential power in the earlier system was the president's control over a large share of the federal budget that was transferred to subnational authorities without either formal rules or predictable criteria. With the tacit consent of the federal Congress (hereafter, the Congress), the president had the ability to make or break state and municipal treasuries.[3]

The emergent plurality of political forces represented in the Congress transformed its rubber-stamp function into a real source of checks and balances on presidential power. Governors from all political parties, including the

2. Domingo (2000).

3. According to Article 40 of the Mexican Constitution, Mexico has a federal system comprising thirty-one states and the federal district (Mexico City). Each state is subdivided into municipalities (currently 2,445).

PRI, were not willing to accept quietly the presidential prerogative of discretionary budget transfers. The pressure from the Congress and the state governors ultimately led the president to relinquish control over a large share of federal expenditures, including his unwritten prerogative of allocating the budget according to his political preferences.

In 1997 the Congress approved new formulas to clarify the transfer of resources from the federal budget to states and municipalities. At the beginning of the 1990s, close to 65 percent of all public spending had been under the control of the federal government. With decentralization, that pattern changed radically: By 2005, 60 cents of each peso of public expenditure was under the control of either state or municipal governments.

The risk of political instability due to budget disputes in the Congress, and an open conflict between state governors and the federal government, was not just a possibility on the horizon but a clear and present danger for the administration of Ernesto Zedillo (1994–2000). Decentralization thus became a mechanism for political survival.[4] The theoretical benefits of decentralization were aligned with the political need to resolve the political and financial disputes between the central government and state governors.

Improved budget transparency had a number of advantages for political actors: Everybody got a slice of the fiscal pie, and everybody knew the size of one's neighbors' slice too. With presidential power shrunk to constitutional size, budget accountability became not only a prerequisite for *good governance* but one of the foundations of the new political stability. To improve government accountability, the Chamber of Deputies redesigned the congressional agency in charge of the oversight of government finances. The *Auditoría Superior de la Federación* (ASF), Mexico's Supreme Audit Institution (SAI), launched its activities in January 2000. This reform increased the operational autonomy and the political independence of the ASF. However, the positive changes in the ASF and other improvements in budget accountability did not spill over to similar improvements at the subnational level.

The interaction between the decline of presidentialism and financial decentralization has triggered a new dynamic of subnational politics in Mexico. Greater political autonomy from the center, increasing financial resources, and a relatively weak system of checks and balances have combined to bolster the power of state governors and municipal presidents. The interaction of democratization and decentralization, within the context of declining presidential power, has brought about unprecedented political and financial autonomy for states and municipalities.

4. Ward and Rodríguez (1999, p. 53).

In several states the governor preserves the habits and informal powers of the former Mexican presidential system. Some state congresses have fulfilled their mission to counterbalance the power of the governor, while in others the checks and balances necessary for a true division of power do not exist. Control over state institutions and the decentralization of spending has given the governors an enormous margin of political and financial power. Meanwhile, the state SAIs, which are supposed to be responsible for enforcing accountability for the more than 60 percent of public funds now spent at regional and local levels, lack the human and financial resources and the institutional autonomy to perform their mission. Each state government has its own methodology and unique standard of breaking down the data on how and by whom public money is spent.

In the *ancien régime,* secrecy over budget data was one of the unwritten prerogatives of the president. The absence (at least in public) of detailed data on government expenditure was one piece of evidence for the preeminence of the executive over the legislative branch. Budget information was inaccessible not only to ordinary citizens and academic researchers but even to members of the opposition in the Congress. Until 1997, when the PRI was defeated in the Chamber of Deputies' elections, the executive did not have any legal or political requirement or incentive to disclose detailed budget information. As with other democratic deficiencies of Mexico's political system, the absence of budget transparency at the federal level also extended to state and municipal authorities. In recent years, the positive steps to build accountability institutions at the federal level, such as a new ASF (the national SAI), the improvements in budget transparency, or the Freedom of Information Act, have not trickled down uniformly to subnational governments. The biggest challenge to Mexico's governance and accountability lies in the modernization of state and municipal governments, under a federal constitutional framework that shields the sovereignty and political autonomy of subnational authorities.

Resolving Constitutional Disputes over Budget Governance

The transition to a *constitutional presidency* left unchanged some crucial areas of budget governance in Mexico. A number of important issues and institutions, which previously were subject to presidential influence but had been left untouched by institutional reform, became the starting point for a political confrontation:

—Did the president have veto power over the federal budget?

—Did the Supreme Audit Institution have the legal right to audit the finances of subnational governments?

—How much of the oil export surplus should be saved and how much allocated for subnational spending? And how should the country project the export price of oil for the purposes of dividing expected public revenues?

During the Vicente Fox presidency (2000–06), these questions became a matter of intense political dispute. The issues were eventually settled by a combination of Supreme Court rulings and the approval of a new law that established the distribution of the nonbudgeted oil surplus between the different levels of government, as well as a formula for forecasting the price of oil.

Establishing the Constitutionality of the Presidential Budget Veto

Somewhere between 87 percent and 93 percent of federal appropriations is made up of committed or earmarked expenditures that are not subject to reallocation.[5] Thus the margin of flexibility in public expenditures is only around 7 to 13 percent of the total budget. In the congressional debate for the 2005 fiscal year, the Chamber of Deputies introduced important modifications to the budget bill. Close to 30 percent of the *soft share* of the budget was modified by the deputies, in line with proposals by a coalition of opposition parties. In response, the president decided to veto the modified share of the budget.

It was a matter of constitutional dispute, however, whether the executive had the legal power to veto the budget. The constitution explicitly allows for a presidential veto of actions approved by both of the two houses of Congress. However, the constitution limits the Senate's role in the budget process exclusively to the approval of government *revenues,* reserving to the Chamber of Deputies the exclusive right to discuss and approve *appropriations.* The Supreme Court had therefore to determine the executive's capacity to veto a bill passed by only a single house. In June 2005, by a split vote of 6 to 5, the Supreme Court ruled that the president had the power to veto the appropriations bill in whole or in part.

For seventy years, the Congress had never dared to modify a single line of the budget without explicit presidential consent. Under the new competitive political system, with presidential power restricted by the law, there had been no clear certainty about the possible outcome of a budget controversy between the Congress and the executive. The Supreme Court ruling strengthened the position of the president on budget matters and filled one of the institutional blanks in Mexico's democratic transition.

5. Fausto Hernández-Trillo of the Centro de Investigacion y Docencia Economicas (CIDE) has used three different sets of variables to calculate the *hard share* of the budget. His calculations produced the following results: depending on the methodology: 87 percent, 91 percent, or 93 percent of the federal budget is not subject to redistribution.

Conflict between the Supreme Audit Institution and State Governments

Article 79 of the constitution establishes the right of the ASF to exercise vertical oversight of federal transfers to states and municipalities. This provision implies that the federal entity has the capacity to supervise the finances of autonomous subnational governments. However, the wording in the constitution, together with some contradictions in secondary legislation, left room for political conflict and judicial interpretation.

Article 2 of the law that regulates the ASF determines that all subnational governments are subject to the oversight authority of the ASF.[6] In contrast, Article 49 of the law, which determines the fiscal relationship between different levels of government, indicates that each of the thirty-two subnational ASFs has the responsibility to perform the ex post audit of the state and municipal governments.[7] However, it was widely recognized that a good number of the subnational ASFs possessed neither the autonomy nor the institutional capacity needed to accept responsibility for the effective audit and accountability of subnational government budgets.

The ASF challenged the prevailing legal framework for not allowing a strict audit process for subnational institutions. Every fiscal year, the ASF would confront several state governments that rejected the federal bureau's financial oversight. The only legal window for the ASF to pursue the audit of decentralized expenditure was to sign cooperation agreements with the state SAIs, although the state congresses were not required to accept such agreements. Even when an agreement was signed, the ASF did not have the legal or political means to enforce it.

In January 2004 the government of the state of Oaxaca and the local congress rejected an audit from the ASF, claiming that it would violate the *Ley de Coordinación Fiscal* and the state's sovereignty. The leader of the local congress stated that "the local SAI cannot audit the expenses of the President of Mexico, so the ASF cannot audit the expenses of the Oaxaca government."[8] This level of political confrontation between the state governors and the ASF was exceptional (although other governors and local congresses had found more subtle ways of obstructing the ASF without receiving much attention from the media). The ASF and the Chamber of Deputies decided to present a constitutional case against the executive and legislative branches of Oaxaca. In

6. *Ley de Fiscalización Superior de la Federación.*

7. *Ley de Coordinación Fiscal.* One for each of the thiry-one state congresses and the Mexico City legislative assembly.

8. *Apro,* "Rechazan en Oaxaca auditoria al Ramo 33," January 27, 2004 (www.proceso.com. mx/noticia.html?nid=21363&cat=2).

August 2006 a unanimous decision of the Supreme Court affirmed that the ASF had the authority to perform an ex post audit of federal transfers used to finance decentralized public services.

Despite being promulgated in 1917, the Mexican Constitution remains young and untried as a legal basis for imposing limits upon political actors.[9] During the years of PRI domination, the executive will rather than the constitution had been the main mechanism for resolving political disputes and the leading source of jurisprudence. With Mexico's recent political transition, the constitution as interpreted by the judiciary has emerged as a new basis for resolving political disputes. In matters of budget governance, as seen in the two cases discussed above, the Supreme Court has become a crucial player in arbitrating conflicts between state branches and the different levels of government.

Sharing the Revenues from Oil

In the uncharted waters of the transition to a constitutional presidency, state governors have pressured the Congress to increase the budget transfers to their regions. The federal deputies became the most important "tax base" for subnational governments, as their lobbying efforts in the Congress were rewarded with sizable budget increases. A large share of these increases came from oil revenues.

Until 2006 Mexico did not have a specific law to manage the surplus from oil revenues. Every year, the Ministry of Finance presented its projections for the average price of a barrel of oil in the revenue side of the budget bill. However, the Congress had the last word over the forecast price per barrel. The price decided has a major impact on the amount of resources available for distribution to states and municipalities. Oil revenues from the national oil company, Pemex, represent on average 35 percent of total government revenues.[10] They also account for close to 48 percent of the pool of transfers to subnational authorities (in turn, close to 90 percent of total subnational spending comes from financial transfers from the federal government).[11]

Following the oil shock of 1998, the executive and the Congress opted to err on the side of caution in their price estimations. From 1999 to 2004, actual year-end market prices were on average 42 percent higher than the budget projections (thus creating an unbudgeted surplus).[12]

9. Silva-Herzog (2004).

10. *Leyes de Ingresos,* 2000–05.

11. This figure of 48 percent was calculated for 2005.

12. Once the projected price is fixed in the Income Law (*Ley de Ingresos*) by both chambers of Congress, the deputies decide how to distribute the potential revenues derived from a positive differential between the projected and observed oil prices.

During the budget approval process for the 2005 fiscal year, there was an unprecedented clash between the two chambers of the Congress over the predictions of the oil price. The Chamber of Deputies ignored the government's cautious proposal to set the expected price at US$23 per barrel, instead settling on US$27 (the highest adjustment the deputies had ever made). Once the deputies changed the price of oil, the Senate received the income bill for its final approval. Before its enactment into law, the senators reversed the price change incorporated by the deputies and reduced the price per barrel to the original figure (US$23) set by the Finance Ministry.

The deputies complained about the lack of coordination between the chambers, but they did not have the legal capacity to overturn the Senate's decision.[13] The calculation of the prospective oil revenues was a not a cold econometric affair but a hotly contested political issue, because of its dramatic impact on the financial balance of state and municipal governments. If subnational authorities could not get additional resources through a higher forecasted oil price, they would aim to obtain a generous share of the potential nonbudgeted oil surplus.

The first priority of the oil surplus has been to cover nonbudgeted governmental expenses that might occur during the fiscal year. In the case of an oil surplus and a higher than expected government deficit, for example, the additional oil revenues would be used to help finance the deficit. Once these unexpected costs had been paid, the remainder of the surplus revenue was distributed according to the guidelines set by the majority consensus of the deputies. As there were no permanent rules to regulate this process, the Chamber of Deputies had to harmonize conflicting interests over the use and allocation of the oil surplus.

In each budget negotiation, the Congress decided the share of the oil surplus to be saved and to be spent. The percentage of distribution of the eventual surplus was then incorporated into the annual federal budget. In 2001, 34 percent of the surplus was allocated for infrastructure projects in Mexico's southern states. For 2003 and 2004, the oil surplus was made available not just to southern states, but to all state governments, and their share of the nonbudgeted oil returns grew to 50 percent. Under the shadow of the oil boom, the price forecast and the distribution of additional revenues became core issues in each year's budget approval process.

---

13. During the weeks of negotiation, the price of oil fell below the US$23 benchmark, reinforcing the argument that price expectations ought to be cautious.

State governors had a special interest in the oil surplus. As it is nonbudgeted revenue, they had greater freedom to allocate the unexpected pool of resources. In most states, the surplus appropriations do not require the approval of the local congress but are merely reported at the end of the fiscal year. So, the oil surplus revenue was managed within a weak framework for oversight and accountability.

To resolve the disputes over the oil price forecast and the distribution of any surplus between levels of government, in March 2006 the Congress approved a new law to establish a statutory framework for the preparation and approval of the budget.[14] The new law created a fixed formula for forecasting oil prices and defined a fixed distribution for prospective oil surpluses:

—25 percent to a stabilization fund for state revenues

—25 percent to a stabilization fund for infrastructure investment by Pemex

—40 percent to a stabilization fund for oil revenues

—10 percent to infrastructure investment in states and municipalities[15]

The Supreme Court decisions and the new legal framework for the federal budget clarified the rules for all the institutional actors involved in the debate and approval of the government's revenue and expenditure.

The Four-Year Budget Cycle

Figure D-1 explains the four-year budget process from its draft and approval (year 1) to its execution (year 2) and the ex post accountability (years 3 and 4) of government accounts at the end of the budget cycle (*Cuenta Pública*).

CSO involvement in the Federal Budget Process

Fundar, a CSO dedicated to budget issues, argues that there is a complete absence of mechanisms for citizen participation in the different stages of the budgetary process.[16] Organizations like Fundar tend to focus on the ex post oversight of government expenditure. In 2004, for example, six CSOs made an audit of spending by the conservative Catholic group Provida, which had received 30 million pesos from the federal budget. Through the Freedom of Information law, these CSOs found that the public money had in fact been used by Provida for different purposes than the announced project of

14. *Ley Federal de Presupuesto y Responsabilidad Hacendaria.*

15. The formula is based on an average of the monthly price of Mexican oil for the previous ten years and the expected future price for the next three years of West Texas oil in the New York Stock Exchange.

16. See, for example, Fundar (2007).

Figure D-1. *Mexico's Federal Budget Cycle*

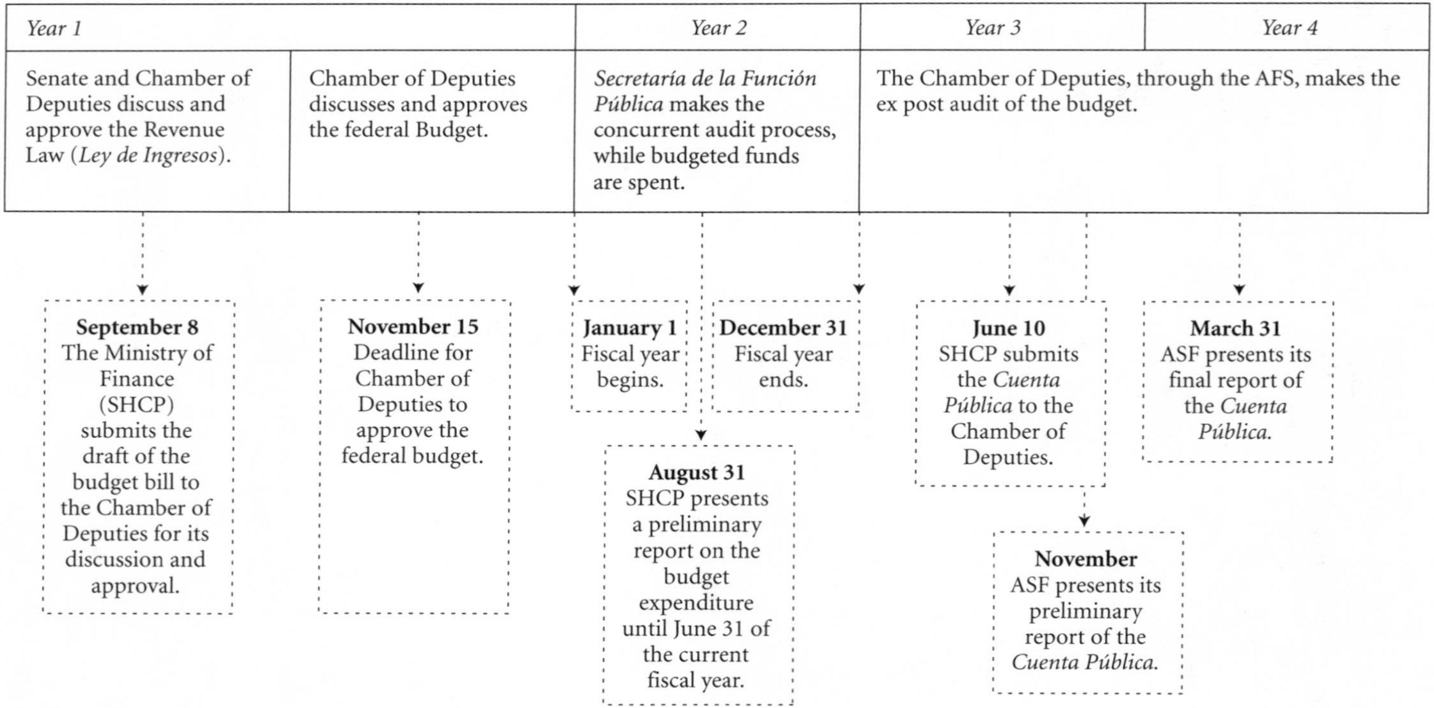

Year 1	Year 2	Year 3	Year 4
Senate and Chamber of Deputies discuss and approve the Revenue Law (*Ley de Ingresos*).	*Secretaría de la Función Pública* makes the concurrent audit process, while budgeted funds are spent.	The Chamber of Deputies, through the AFS, makes the ex post audit of the budget.	
Chamber of Deputies discusses and approves the federal Budget.			

September 8
The Ministry of Finance (SHCP) submits the draft of the budget bill to the Chamber of Deputies for its discussion and approval.

November 15
Deadline for Chamber of Deputies to approve the federal budget.

January 1
Fiscal year begins.

December 31
Fiscal year ends.

August 31
SHCP presents a preliminary report on the budget expenditure until June 31 of the current fiscal year.

June 10
SHCP submits the *Cuenta Pública* to the Chamber of Deputies.

March 31
ASF presents its final report of the *Cuenta Pública*.

November
ASF presents its preliminary report of the *Cuenta Pública*.

constructing clinics for assistance to pregnant women. One public servant was sanctioned and banned from working in government as a consequence of this CSO review. This example represented a pioneering case of civil society involvement in the governance of public expenditure.

Role of the Media

The analysis of budget transparency in Mexico is a novel exercise, which started in the last years of the 1990s. The enactment in 2002 of the Freedom of Information Act has become a powerful tool for journalists' research on budget transparency.[17] National newspapers now perform a relevant role in the accountability of federal government expenditure. In addition to journalists' own in-house work on budget issues, newspapers are very receptive to publishing the findings of think tanks, CSOs, or academics who conduct budget expenditure research. In this regard, the press has become the most active arena for exchanging signals and actions between citizens and the public sector. Despite the fact that most of the Mexican population does not read newspapers devoted to hard news, the information carried by serious newspapers generates a spillover effect into the electronic media, such as radio and TV news programs, that pick up newspaper stories and make them accessible to the general public.

The CSO and the media have helped to create a weak, but strengthening, critical mass around the issue of budget efficiency. This critical mass has sent constant signals about the growth of current government spending, the increasing cost of the bureaucracy, and waste and corruption at all three levels of government. The public sector has begun to acknowledge these challenges, and has started to take some steps to address issues concerning budget efficiency and accountability.

Special Interests

There is anecdotal evidence of special interest groups trying to defend either privileges in taxing policies or benefits through subsidies and apportions programs. However, there is, as yet, no systematic research on the role and influence of special interests in the preparation and approval of the government budget.

Closing the De Jure–De Facto Gap

For most of the twentieth century, there was a wide gap between the de jure and de facto powers of different public institutions. The transition to a constitutional presidency has led to a closing of this gap. The Congress has

---

17. *Ley Federal Transparencia y Acceso a la Información.*

become the central forum for the budget approval process and has acquired the authority to perform its oversight role by means of approving and auditing public expenditure. At the same time, though, the Supreme Court's validation of the presidential right of veto over the budget has given the executive a new formal power over budget governance. The court's ruling has given enhanced certainty to the rules of the budget process, and this has reduced the level of confrontation between the executive and the Congress.

Outlook

The scale and the technical complexity of the federal budget have limited the engagement of citizens and CSOs in the ex ante oversight of the federal government. Institutions like Fundar have had some success in the area of the ex post accountability of government expenditure. There is still wide room for stronger CSO oversight of the federal budget, although the biggest challenge and opportunity for civil society engagement now rests in active participation in state and municipal budget accountability.

On June 2007, the Congress approved a reform of Article 6 of the Constitution, which requires states and municipalities to consider all the information under their control as freely accessible to the public unless classified otherwise under terms established by the new law. This constitutional reform should help trigger new levels of transparency where it matters the most to citizens: at the local level.

The preparation and approval of state and municipal budgets offer wide opportunities for citizen participation. The constitutional affirmation of the freedom of information holds the potential to bring about a major cultural change in Mexican society. The Freedom of Information Law already has had a wide impact: since 2003 there have been 237,000 information requests. This represents a real transformation in a country where government information was previously the exclusive possession of politicians and bureaucrats.

Most public spending, however, now takes places at the subnational level. To transform institutional reform into cultural change, it will be necessary to support citizen initiatives that aim to use the Freedom of Information Law to promote budget accountability in local communities. Civil society engagement at the municipal level has huge potential. Increased budget transparency could translate into more productive and efficient public expenditure. Cultural change will occur when citizens relate a more accountable budget to a positive effect on their quality of life.

References

Domingo, Pilar. 2000. "Judicial Independence: The Politics of the Supreme Court in Mexico." *Journal of Latin American Studies* 32, no. 3: 705–35.

Fundar. 2007. *Índice Latinoamericano de transparencia presupuestaria: estudio sobre México.* Mexico City.

Lujambio, Alonso. 1995. *Federalismo y Congreso en el Cambio Político de México.* Mexico City: UNAM-Instituto de Investigaciones Jurídicas.

Silva-Herzog, Jesús. 2004. "Mexico: Problems of a New Democracy." Lecture given at the Center for Latin American Studies. University of Chicago, October 21 (http://chiasmos.uchicago.edu/events/silva-herzog.shtml).

Ward, Peter M., and Victoria E. Rodríguez. 1999. "New Federalism, Intra-Governmental Relations and Co-Governance in Mexico." *Journal of Latin American Studies* 31, no. 3: 673–710.

BJOERN DRESSEL

E

Transparency and Accountability in Thailand's Budget Process

Historical Governance Context

Thailand is the only country in Southeast Asia that was never colonized. Rather than having Western institutions forced on it, the country gradually became open to them under a modernizing monarchy in the nineteenth century. As a result of the limited direct, external influence, many traditional structures are still in place: the unchallenged authority of the monarchy, the role of the Buddhist Sangha (monastic order), and the dominance of the bureaucracy, both military and civilian. The most recent constitution describes the country as a parliamentary democracy with a constitutional monarchy and unitary administration. Since the 1960s a vigorous middle class and an active civil society have emerged. Thailand's system of governance is now being challenged to accommodate new and old.

Thailand seemed to adopt democracy as early as 1932, when young army and civilian officers staged a coup against the absolute monarchy, but for decades appearances of democracy were largely illusory. Royalists, civil servants, and the military continued to vie with each other for control under what became known as a "bureaucratic polity."[1] Between 1932 and the mid-1990s, Thailand experienced at least twenty military coups, more than fifty cabinets, and fifteen constitutions, as the country passed through vicious cycles of elections, instability, and military coups. The pattern of governance, for the most part, was at best semidemocratic. Political institutionalization

1. Riggs (1966).

was low because of the frequency of coups, the discontinuity of parliaments, and the weakness of political parties.

Since the 1960s, however, rapid economic growth and modernization have had their effect. There has emerged an increasingly assertive class of businesspeople who have sought more active involvement in politics, first through alliances with bureaucrats and later by forming clientelistic or charismatic political parties. The effects were clearly negative in the 1980s when, profiting from political liberalization, politicians with business backgrounds turned cabinet positions into personal pork barrels and plundered the public budget.[2] At the same time, though, there arose civil society and middle-class constituencies, which became the catalyst for mass democratic demands, first in 1973 and more successfully in 1992.[3]

As the influence of the military waned, and with the implicit support of the king, Thailand has since moved toward a formal liberal democratic system. The growing influence of civil society was particularly illustrated in the 1997 constitution, the first democratically drafted constitution in Thai history, which produced an institutional framework that explicitly intended to enhance stability, encourage popular participation, and promote good governance.

Yet over the last decade, it has become clear that democratic governance in Thailand remains fragile. Under the government of Prime Minister Thaksin Shinawatra (2001–06), the new constitution, while supporting new degrees of government stability and effectiveness, did little to prevent the government from abusing its power and interfering with the independence of the new oversight agencies, undermining the rule of law, and engaging in nontransparent practices, widely perceived as corrupt.[4] Moreover, another military intervention in September 2006, after weeks of standoff between the government and largely urban, middle-class protesters, led to the ouster of the elected Shinawatra government and the installation of a transitional military government. The latter committed itself to a return to democracy within a year, but a ban on the prime minister's former political party was among the elements that called into question the nature of the political system that would emerge.[5]

2. Phongpaichit and Baker (1998).
3. Hewison (1997); Wyatt (2003).
4. Phongpaichit and Baker (2005).
5. Elections held in December 2007 resulted in a six-party coalition's being formed by the new People Power Party, itself widely seen as a replacement vehicle for the interests and allies of former Prime Minister Thaksin Shinawatra, who remained personally banned from public office. Political life in Thailand continued to be turbulent throughout 2008. (*Editor*).

Thailand's governance context is best understood against the background of a rapidly modernizing political entity that has seen the emergence of new social actors seeking political accommodation. The impact of the Asian financial crisis (1997–98) was critical; it temporarily weakened many of Thailand's traditional elites, allowing new actors—many of them from civil society—to push for enlarged political participation and to highlight good governance. But too many critical governance issues remained unresolved: the continuous divide between urban economic power centers and the rural areas where most voters live; the uneasy accommodation of religious and ethnic minorities, which fuel the Muslim insurgency in the south; or the future role of the monarchy itself, whose legitimacy and influence seem stronger than ever but whose institutional role beyond the reign of much-revered King Bhumipol Adulyadej (Rama IX) seems uncertain. Certainly, the 2006 coup suggests that Thailand's traditional elites are not yet ready to accept democratic governance if it produces outcomes they deem undesirable.

As recent developments demonstrate, an analysis of governance dynamics in Thailand needs to account for formal and informal patterns of power and accountability. A closer look at the budget process will underline this point.

Diagnosis

Thailand's budgeting process has traditionally been a highly opaque, top-down exercise with little public input. Structured by long-standing legal rules designed to constrain the impact of political pressures and maintain a high degree of technocratic insulation, the budget process has continued to be highly centralized and hierarchical.

Principal Actors

The central government spends about 85 percent of total general expenditures and collects 95 percent of general tax revenues. A limited number of actors operate within clearly defined constraints designed to foster fiscal discipline.[6] For instance, although formally assigned to the cabinet, budget preparation since the 1960s has been driven by the "Gang of Four" macroeconomic lead agencies:

—*The Bank of Thailand,* responsible for formulating monetary policy and maintaining monetary stability, by supervising financial institutions, for example

---

6. Samudavanija (1971, 1990); Dhiravegin and Dhiratayakinant (1987).

—*The Ministry of Finance (MOF)*, responsible for collecting government revenue and managing macroeconomic policy primarily through its fiscal policy office, as well as overseeing the operation of about eleven state-owned enterprises

—The *National Economic and Social Development Board (NESDB)*, the central planning agency that studies the Thai economy and draws up annual and five-year plans and appraises development projects; and coordinates, monitors, and evaluates their implementation

—The *Bureau of the Budget (BOB)*, patterned in 1959 after the U.S. Office of Management and Budget, sited in the Office of the Prime Minister, responsible for formulating the annual budget and overseeing departmental budget preparation, while also approving its implementation

Led by BOB, these agencies would get together in closed meetings to prepare the budget. Once the budget was approved by the cabinet (a formality), BOB would review and approve requests for the release of funds and then monitor results. In addition to the Gang of Four, the Ministry of Interior, acting through its Department of Local Administration and Community Development, authorized disbursements by districts and subdistricts through a representative reporting directly to the governor of the province. This closed technocratic process is generally thought to have guaranteed Thailand's good track record in aggregate fiscal discipline.

Parliament, despite its power of the purse, has had little to do with the budget process. Within a British Westminster-style parliamentary system, executive control over parliament has been quite high, and several laws have limited the role of parliament and reinforced the role of the executive. For instance, in a constitutional provision carried through since the 1960s, parliament can decrease but cannot increase the ceilings in a budget bill. Furthermore, the Budget Procedure Act of 1959 limits deficit financing to 20 percent of the annual budget and 80 percent of the budget earmarked for debt repayment. The same law also mandates that the Budget Scrutiny Committee (BSC), an ad hoc committee for the second reading of a budget bill, be chaired by the minister of finance, with the budget director serving as secretary. As an ad hoc committee, the BSC has no permanent research staff, making it dependent on the expertise of the Budget Bureau. While this has not prevented the BSC from becoming the traditional stage for efforts by members of parliament to influence budget allocations through logrolling across party lines, the rules have clearly reduced parliament's ability to change the executive proposal.

Given this technocratic process, it is not surprising that external actors, such as supreme audit institutions and civil society, have had little influence on the budget. For instance, although internal audit agencies such as the Department of the Comptroller General have been influential, the structural affiliation of the National Audit Office with the prime minister's office has constrained its independence.[7] Similarly, representatives of business or non-governmental organizations have had virtually no formal channels for influencing the budget process and have therefore relied on the use of informal channels and public protest to influence budget outcomes. A notable exception has been the royal court (including the Privy Council), which—despite having no formal role—has at times exerted considerable influence over development strategies and budget allocations.

Although in essence the budgetary process and actors have remained virtually unchanged for the last quarter century, there have been a few notable changes. For instance, in the mid-1980s the government started to experiment more openly with neo-corporatist arrangements—a joint Public and Private Sector Consultative Committee, closer cooperation with think tanks, and more open consultation between NESDB and NGOs as the five-year development plans were drafted. At times, parliament has scrutinized the executive's budget, although its engagement has fluctuated widely.

The Asian financial crisis and the drafting of a new constitution in 1997 probably provided the most profound impetus for major change in the governance of the budget. As the crisis forced the government to react to international concerns and make budget and financial information more transparent, the constitution provided the institutional framework for greater transparency, accountability, and participation. For instance, the 1997 constitution established a National Advisory Council on Economic and Social Affairs to advise the Cabinet, bringing together experts and business and civil society activists. It also created an independent Office of the Auditor General and gave new constitutional guarantees for participation of the media and civil society in the political process. The deliberate attempt to strengthen political parties and the role of the executive and the cabinet also provided opportunities for political actors to establish greater control over the bureaucratic lead agencies. Finally, the planned decentralization would have transferred considerably greater budgetary autonomy to the local level over the next years.

In the end, though, many of the intended innovations did not transpire, either because the political leadership was determined to undermine them or because of stiff resistance from the bureaucracy. Hence, traditional patterns

7. Medhi Krongkaew (1990).

Figure E-1. *Budget Process in Thailand: Signals and Actions*

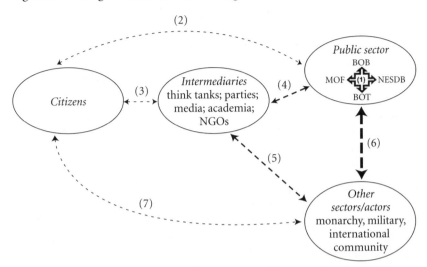

have held sway. A closer look at accountability routes in Thailand's budget process may clarify this point.

Signals and Actions in the Budget Process

Figure E-1 tries to capture critical agent relationships in Thailand's budget process, highlighting key actors and the strength of their relationships (marked by the thickness of the arrows).

Taking budget demands as signals and the budget proposal as action, the following patterns can be identified in Thailand's budget process:

—*Intrabureaucratic, Route 1.* The Gang of Four still exerts great influence on the budget process. Claiming high technocratic expertise, these agencies generally engage in closed meeting budget planning between November and March of each year. They must reconcile signals from a variety of political actors, the public, or the bureaucracy itself within the five-year development plan and the general economic situation. The process is facilitated by the amount of bureaucratic insulation, which in turn reflects the traditional meritocratic selection of bureaucrats, with their primary loyalty being to the royal court rather than to the political class, and the tradition of fiscal prudence that persists in these agencies. Given the political volatility of Thai governance, it should not be surprising that the bureaucrats provide much-needed stability and continuity in developmental planning, functioning as a counterbalance to the potential for the political class to abuse public resources, for example, by distorting signals from the public. However, the technocratic agencies stand accused of sending strong signals on their own by traditionally emphasizing policies of growth over those of greater equity.[8] Public sector reforms under the Thaksin government attempted to establish greater control over the bureaucratic agencies by reducing the influence of NESDB in the design of five-year plans and considering moving BOB under the MOF. Although this potentially might be justified on grounds of greater bureaucratic efficiency, the opinion of many that this was a deliberate attempt to reduce the technocratic counterweight in policymaking seemed to be confirmed by the 208 percent budget increase for the prime minister's office from the 2001 to 2004 fiscal years. Given recent developments, the future of these reforms remains to be seen.

—*Citizens–Public Sector, Route 2.* The flow of signals and actions between citizens and the public administration has been minimal for several reasons. The most obvious is that Thailand has traditionally suffered from a deeply flawed electoral process marked by candidate buying, canvasser recruitment, vote buying, and official corruption, especially in rural areas.[9] Political parties are weak, and collective action is unusual in rural areas, where the majority of the electorate lives. As a result, voters' budget preferences have usually been highly distorted. Moreover, the unitary state structure and an insulated bureaucracy offer few entry points for local citizen demands; there is no incentive for bureaucrats to be more responsive, while the hierarchical Thai culture stresses deference to authority. Nevertheless, there have been some notable changes in this route. The growth of NGOs, rural as well as urban, has helped overcome collective action problems and put pressure on the administration to react to citizen concerns. Similarly, recent constitutional and electoral law changes have reinforced electoral accountability by reducing vote buying and fostering the emergence of more stable, and possibly more programmatic, parties. Recent social policies under the Thaksin Shinwatra government (for example, the 30 baht health care scheme, Village Fund, and so on) are a case in point. With a voter base mainly among the rural and urban poor, the Thaksin government was far more responsive to voter demands than other governments were in the past, though many soon had questions about the sustainability of its populist policies.

—*Citizens-Intermediary, Route 3.* The link between citizens and intermediary agents in terms of the budget process is also fragile for a number of reasons. The majority of intermediaries, whether they are think tanks, media,

8. Muscat (1994); Unger (2003).
9. Phongpaichit and Piriyarangsan (1996).

or NGOs, still cater primarily to urban audiences. Also, while think tanks such as the Thailand Development Research Institute and academic research institutions within settings such as the National Institute for Development Administration, Chulalongkorn University, and Thammasat University have turned more attention to the budget, little information is distributed beyond the academic and urban community. The media sector is heavily regulated and controlled by the state (three TV stations are owned by the military), and with few exceptions, the print media lack the technical expertise (and perhaps the will) to inform the public comprehensively about the budget. Finally, the NGO community, despite its considerable growth, has traditionally focused on local issues and has only over the last decade turned to such broader issues as reform of education, health care, or the legal system. The budget watchers found elsewhere are absent from the Thai context. Hence, except for an occasional sporadic mobilization resulting from a highly publicized abuse of public finances, few signals and actions flow through this route.

—*Intermediary–Public Sector, Route 4.* The relationships of some intermediaries with the public sector itself, by contrast, seem to be moderately strong. Since the mid-1980s, Thai governments have increasingly promoted neo-corporatist arrangements not only with business but also with NGOs, as illustrated by the NGO coordinating committee on rural development set up in 1985. Recognizing the sector's growing role in the development process, NESDB started in the mid-1990s to hold regular consultations with NGOs as it prepared the five-year plans. Similarly, the government regularly consults research institutions and think tanks on issues related to development planning and budget reform, although many believe that the bureaucracy at times has a bias toward foreign advice. The new ability to move from the bureaucracy into academic positions and vice versa has also strengthened this route, though such transfers remain the exception rather than the rule (unlike in parts of East Asia).

—*The Role of Other Actors, Routes 5, 6, and 7.* Paradoxically, some of the least formal routes see more signal and action flows. This applies in particular to the royal court, which can claim unquestioned authority over the public sector actors, who remain royal appointees first and public servants only second. Given the legitimacy of the current king, there is little doubt about the court's influence over intermediary actors and the general public; the many charitable royal organizations also ensure that signals flow back in the reverse direction (albeit to a much lesser extent). Although the influence of the military had until recently been waning, it has continued to influence the policy process through its control of the media and its close linkages to the monarchy and the bureaucratic class even as it has lost legitimacy among citizens and some NGOs. Finally, there is the international community (understood to include international financial institutions and bilateral donors), whose influence became prominent during the Asian financial crisis (much to the dismay of the ruling elites). While the recent economic recovery has reduced the role of the international community, it has done much, often in conjunction with the international business community, to encourage the provision of transparent information on financial and fiscal information and to exert pressure for transparent and accountable governance.

As shown in this brief analysis, the flow of signals and actions in the budget process differs dramatically among the different routes, some of which are not formally institutionalized. Unlike other governance changes Thailand has undergone over the last decade, the budget process is still patterned on structures known from the classic bureaucratic polity. Transparency, accountability, and participation are limited.

Hence, there is considerable space for civil society to actively reinforce some of the linkages. To do this, it would be necessary inter alia to build better channels for information between citizens and intermediary actors by publishing understandable and useful information about the budget process, build the capacity of CSOs to participate in developmental planning and budgeting, and join forces with institutions of accountability—the new Office of the Auditor General and parliamentary budget committees.

The past provides a number of successful examples to build upon. In March 1996 NGOs pushed NESDB to agree to regional consultations on the People's Development Plan, which formed the basis for the eighth five-year development plan and set the standard for future practice. It validated the role of CSOs in constitutional reform, ensured that free education and health care became enshrined in the constitution, and prefigured new social policies designed to allocate resources more equitably and, more generally, to give more emphasis to equity vis-à-vis technocratic growth policies. CSOs could also become increasingly important if decentralization finally moves ahead, provided they build their own capacity and exploit the new formal channels of accountability.

Outlook

Involving civil society in Thailand's budget process is a major challenge. Capacity is weak among critical CSO actors, partly because of the antagonism of traditional actors to greater public involvement. Nevertheless, Thailand's

NGOs have become increasingly important within the budget process and the public discourse surrounding it. Social policies—health, education, and rural development—have traditionally been the main concern of the Thai NGO sector.[10] What is needed now is a commitment by CSOs to transmit budget information to the public and to ensure that accountability mechanisms, whether vertical or horizontal, become more effective. Only then will there be meaningful change in budgetary governance in Thailand.

Donors and other external organizations can support the process by keeping pressure on the Thai government for transparent and accountable budget practices and helping create capacity among the oversight agencies as well as within the NGO community so that the budget is formulated in a more open and participatory way. Although the reputation of the international community suffered during the Asian financial crisis, its expertise is still in high demand and willingly received, which should be seen as an opportunity for future interventions.

In short, building up civil society capacity so that it can actually influence the budget is critical for the future. Although recent turmoil may have temporarily put budget issues aside, it should be remembered that the 2006 political crisis was triggered above all by the allegations of executive abuse of public resources and policy corruption. It was CSOs that mobilized public support for the ouster of Prime Minister Thaksin Shinawatra, which makes it unlikely for them to step back into the shadows.

In sum, the next five to ten years will provide challenges and opportunities alike. There are major issues related to greater civil society engagement in the budget, which is critical to governance in Thailand (and everywhere else). Besides building CSO capacity, there is also a need to reach out more to citizens beyond the urban centers and gradually change bureaucratic practices and attitudes about public involvement. Paradoxically, the Thaksin period could provide a model: it helped mobilize constituencies among the rural and urban poor that had previously been neglected in the political process. Now they are aware of the implications and possibilities of greater electoral accountability for public policy. The challenge is to help them realize those possibilities.

References

Boonyarattanasoontorn, Jaturong, and Gawin Chutima. 1995. *Thai NGOs: The Continuing Struggle for Democracy.* Bangkok: Thai NGO Support Project.

10. Boonyarattanasoontorn and Chutima (1995); Robb (2002); Simpkins (2003).

Dhiravegin, Likhit, and Kraiyudht Dhiratayakinant. 1987. *Allocation for Development: The Role of the Budget Bureau.* Report 3. Bangkok: United Nations Development Programme.

Hewison, Kevin, ed. 1997. *Political Change in Thailand: Democracy and Participation.* London and New York: Routledge.

Krongkaew, Medhi. 1990. "The Management and Control of Government Expenditures in Thailand."

Muscat, Robert J. 1994. *The Fifth Tiger: A Study of Thai Development Policy.* Armonk, N.Y.: United Nations University Press; M. E. Sharpe.

Phongpaichit, Pasuk, and Chris Baker. 1998. *Thailand's Boom and Bust.* Chiang Mai, Thailand: Silkworm Books.

———. 2005. "Business Populism in Thailand." *Journal of Democracy* 16, no. 2: 58–72.

Phongpaichit, Pasuk, and Sungsidh Piriyarangsan. 1996. *Corruption and Democracy in Thailand.* Chiang Mai, Thailand: Silkworm Books.

Riggs, F. 1966. *Thailand: The Modernization of a Bureaucratic Polity.* Honolulu: East-West Center.

Robb, Caroline M. 2002. *Can the Poor Influence Policy?* 2nd ed. Washington: World Bank and International Monetary Fund.

Samudavanija, Chai Anan. 1971. *The Politics and Administration of the Thai Budgetary Process.* Ph.D. dissertation, University of Wisconsin.

———. 1990. "Economic Policy-Making in a Liberal Technocratic Polity." In *Economic Policy Making in the Asia-Pacific Region,* edited by J. W. Langford and L. K. Brownsey. Halifax, Nova Scotia: The Institute for Research on Public Policy.

Simpkins, Dulcey. 2003. "Radical Influence on the Third Sector: Thai N.G.O. Contributions to Socially Responsive Politics." In *Radicalising Thailand: New Political Perspectives,* edited by Ji Giles Ungpakorn. Bangkok: Institute of Asian Studies, Chulalongkorn University.

Unger, Danny. 2003. "Principals of the Thai State." In *Reinventing Leviathan: The Politics of Administrative Reform in Developing Countries,* edited by B. Ross Schneider and B. Heredia. Miami: North-West Center at the University of Miami.

Wyatt, David K. 2003. *Thailand: A Short History.* 2nd ed. Chiang Mai, Thailand: Silkworm Books.

Four Composite Country Cases of Attempted Governance Reforms

The four examples are composites, based on the authors' years of working with and observing more than sixty countries in Africa, Asia, and Latin America.

Example 1

An African country had just had a regime change, with the new head of state committing to fairer, more effective government that would deliver better results more reliably. Dedicated reformers within government, bolstered by broad backing from constituents and eager support from donors and external advisers, dug into their work. Actions were taken that seemed assured of ending the misdeeds of the past, through drawing on successful measures from other countries. After a year, indicators of progress showed no improvement (for example, the Transparency International Corruption Index remained unchanged), but the politicians and their supporters, fearful of failure, found refuge in declamations about how major transformations would take time. After two years, with still no improvement, everyone moved on to other issues, and the plan for better government was quietly forgotten.

Later, evidence confirmed that the actions taken, and the advice they were based on, implicitly assumed that the country was an institutionalized democracy with strong participatory processes, as the external experts would have liked it to be and as their textbooks and own-country experience had led them to favor. The reforms presumed that once the country's citizenry had more complete information about what the government was doing, the wheels of democratic machinery would take care of the rest, shining a light on

173

problems and facilitating the fixing of them. In fact, however, the country's democratic procedures coexisted with, and were overshadowed by, a longer-standing tradition of leader-dominated governance, under which the head of state and the team around him exercised vast sway over everything. As a result, striving to get more information into citizens' hands could not have much impact because citizens were reluctant to rock the boat, or could not, even if they tried. The media, though supposedly free from government control, had learned to avoid issues that could get them into trouble. Political opposition voices had learned not to step over certain lines. Voters had learned to stick with the incumbent. In short, problems that would have been regime-toppling scandals in textbook-perfect institutionalized democracies failed to get traction in this country's mixed combination of governance structures.

This first example underscores the failure to perform a diagnosis before issuing a prescription. The reformers and their external helpers introduced solutions from elsewhere without considering the special features of this particular country's situation and adapting their plans accordingly.

Example 2

A Latin American country ran afoul of another error—failure to analyze and therefore treat the underlying conditions. The reformers, in this second case, knew from experience their country's unique mix of governance structures and dismissed the initial misguided notions of the external advisers. Although the problems were understood at the outset, the remedies were nevertheless ill-chosen.

The reformers knew that one problem that needed addressing was a lack of transparency in the public sector: Government agencies were releasing too little information, and the paltry amount that saw the light of day was of poor quality. Unfortunately, the sole remedy adopted was freedom of information legislation without strong enforcement to ensure compliance.

The reformers knew that simply releasing more raw information would not be enough: the information would then have to be transmitted into a more digestible form, so that citizens could grasp the core messages and make use of them. The reformers further knew that this change required a steady stream of analyses of the information, and that, while government bodies could do some of that, entities unconnected with the government would need to be able to do some analysis too, if citizens were to feel that the results were credible. But having got that far, the reformers did not seek to eliminate the formidable barriers that kept groups outside government from getting full information and feeling free to disseminate their conclusions.

The reformers knew that voting was critical to getting citizens to exercise more vigorously their right to participate in the processes that capture and convey their voice and their views. However, they did not explore why voting and other forms of citizen participation were limited. Had they done so, they would have come up against the fact that certain groups, by ethnicity and income level, were impeded by significant barriers from participating in their country's political system.

No less important, the reformers knew that the instruments of interaction between citizens and their government included top-down actions (for example, government passes a law), bottom-up actions (citizens' groups lobby for a policy change), and sideways actions (peer pressure, as when hospitals compare themselves with how other hospitals are performing). But they did not take the further step of exploring in detail which specific possible actions within these categories merited the most attention, given the potential benefits and the costs of change.

In this second example, even though the initial diagnosis was insightful, it was not sufficiently thorough. The failure to address the fundamental interactions of citizens and government resulted in missed opportunities for identifying appropriate remedies.

Example 3

An Asian country that avoided the pitfalls that bedeviled the previous two cases nevertheless stumbled. A lack of consensus regarding priorities and a failure to address entrenched resistance to reform revealed and even exacerbated weaknesses.

First, as the reformers moved from diagnosis to prescription, disagreements emerged among them and with others outside the reform team, in the legislature, and elsewhere. Some were disturbed that while the reforms had some chance of improving the effectiveness and efficiency of government agencies, they would do little for improving equity generally or providing better public services for the poor in particular. Others complained that battling corruption was getting short shrift.

Second, although most of those involved recognized that special interest groups would continue, in any system, to try to win advantages for themselves and subvert whatever new initiatives were introduced, few understood that a potential adverse effect of introducing any particular reform aimed at leveling the playing field might be to push special interests to discover inadvertently new, more devious ways to circumvent the system. And few understood that the net result of pressing on one front might be to drive undesired behaviors underground, where they would be harder to expose and possibly more damaging in the end.

Ultimately, the disagreements over priorities and the failure to disarm special interests' remedies led to a mixture of weak reforms so that change for the better was much less than anticipated. Efficiency, effectiveness, equity, relief of poverty, honesty, sustainability, and other possible objectives were left as vague notions, with no consensus on the priorities among them. Furthermore, lack of attention to the constant efforts by special interests to game the system to their profit exposed the reform effort to risks of doing more unintended harm than planned good.

What went wrong in this third example is that the overall goals of the reform effort were not agreed upon in advance, and special interests were able to exploit change. There was debate, but no resolution; meanwhile, special interests went unchecked.

Example 4

The last example illustrates the fallacy of seizing on corruption as the sole source of all government failings. In this case, however, the response to a righteous public outcry was an investigation that, in turn, revealed underlying complexities and offered evidence that could lead to specific, efficacious reforms.

A middle-income country's reformers set out to stamp out corruption, motivated by media and public outcry over one too many excesses. Focusing on reports that money appropriated by the legislature for a particular purpose at public hospitals appeared to have no impact on the hospital's services, the reformers set out to find who had made off with all the money. When the investigation results came back, two factors explained everything.

First, the hospitals had no ability at all to distinguish this money from all the other government money they received. Given that, and the fact that the hospitals' management was under relentless pressure and in constant chaos just to get from one day to the next as doctors and nurses concentrated on patients, not on accounting for the funds received and spent, the specially appropriated money was being lumped in with all of the hospitals' other funds and used for whatever was the most urgent need of the moment.

Second, the executive branch of the government had not released all the appropriated money, preferring, for macroeconomic management reasons, to restrain total government spending.

So, a certain amount of public money was not being used for its intended purpose, but the cause was not corruption in the sense of diversion of public money for private use. No individuals were enriching themselves. No smoking-gun evidence allowed the leveling of fraud or abuse charges. Rather, two systemic problems of an entirely different nature were to blame. One had to do with hospital management capabilities and competing demands among priorities. The other had to do with the perennial tension between legislative and executive branches about the right level of government spending.

The main point of this final example is that although corruption is not always the biggest part, and sometimes may be only a small part, if at all, of problems that arise in the implementation of a policy or program, its investigation may reveal other errors in need of a remedy. If implementation is an extensive chain of links from the launching of a reform to its final evaluation, then weaknesses along the way may include systemic conflicts in government functions, management deficiencies, honest incompetence, and more. If, however, the media and monitoring groups have sufficient clout to enable an investigation to proceed and its results to be publicized, then corruption and other underlying malfunctions can be exposed.

List of Acronyms

ACC	Anti-Corruption Campaign Commission
AIDS	Acquired immune deficiency syndrome
APRM	African Peer Review Mechanism
ASF	Auditoría Superior de la Federación
BOB	Bureau of the Budget
BOT	Bank of Thailand
BRAC	Bangladesh Relief Assistance Committee
BSC	Budget Scrutiny Committee
CAG	Controller and Auditor General
CBA	Centre for Budget Advocacy
CBK	Central Bank of Kenya
CDF	Constituency Development Fund
CEPA	Centre for Policy Analysis
CFAA	Country Financial Accountability Assessments
CG	Consultative group
CPAR	Country Procurement Assessment Reports
CPI	Corruption Perceptions Index
CSO	Civil society organization
DCG	Department of the Comptroller General
DfID	Department for International Development
DNPP	National Directorate for Public Budget
DPs	development partners
EU	European Union
FAAC	Fiscal Analysis and Appropriations Committee
FM	frequency modulation

FOI	Freedom of information
GCB	Global Corruption Barometer report
GCI	Global Competitiveness Index
GDP	Gross domestic product
GII	Ghana Integrity Initiative
GITS	Government Information Technology Services
GLSS	Ghana Living Standards Survey
GNECC	Ghana National Education Campaign Coalition
GoG	Government of Ghana
GPRS I	Ghana Poverty Reduction Survey
GPRS II	Growth and Poverty Reduction Strategy
GSS	Ghana Statistical Service
HDI	Human Development Index
HIPC	Heavily indebted poor countries
HIV	Human immunodeficiency virus
HPI	Human Poverty Index
HWP	HIPC Watch Project
IADB	Inter-American Development Bank
IAS	Indian Administrative Service
IBP	International Budget Partnership
ICS	Indian Civil Service
IDEG	Institute for Democratic Governance
IEA	Institute of Economic Affairs
IFE	Instituto Federal Electoral
IFES	International Foundation for Electoral Systems
IFI	International financial institution
IMF	International Monetary Fund
IMO	Independent monitoring organization
IPA	Institute for Policy Alternatives
IRI	International Republican Institute
ISODEC	Integrated Social Development Centre
ISSER	Institute of Statistical, Social, and Economic Research
JPPSCC	Joint Public and Private Sector Consultative Committee
KACC	Kenya Anti-Corruption Commission
KAM	Kenya Association of Manufacturers
KANU	Kenya African National Union
KEPSA	Kenya Private Sector Alliance
KIPRA	Kenya Institute for Public Policy and Research Analysis
KRA	Kenya Revenue Authority

MCA	Millennium Challenge Account
MDAs	Ministries, departments, and agencies
MDBS	Multi Donor Budget Support
MDRI	Multilateral Debt Relief Initiative
MMDAs	Metropolitan, municipal, and district assemblies
MOF	Ministry of Finance
MoFEP	Ministry of Finance and Economic Planning
MOI	Ministry of Interior
MP	Member of parliament
MTEF	Medium-Term Expenditure Framework
MWG	Macroeconomic working group
NARC	National Rainbow Coalition
NDC	National Democratic Congress
NDI	National Democratic Institute
NESC	National Economic and Social Council
NESDB	National Economic and Social Development Board
NGO	Nongovernmental organization
NGO-COD	Nongovernmental organization–coordinating committee on rural development
NIDA	National Institute for Development Administration
NNED	Northern Network for Education and Development
NOA	National Audit Office
NPP	New Patriotic Party
OAG	Office of the Auditor General
OBI	Open Budget Index
OECD	Organization for Economic Cooperation and Development
PAC	Public Accounts Committee
PETS	Public expenditure tracking surveys
PIC	Public Investment Committee
PISA	Programme for International Student Assessment
PM	Prime minister
PPMED	Policy Planning, Monitoring, and Evaluation Departments
PPP	purchasing power parity
PRI	Institutional Revolutionary Party, or *Partido Revolucionario Institucional*
PRSP	Poverty Reduction Strategy Paper
SAI	Supreme Audit Institution
SEND	Social Enterprise Development Foundation of West Africa

SHCP	Secretaría de Hacienda y Crédito Público
SWGs	Sectoral working groups
TDRI	Thailand Development Research Institute
TI	Transparency International
TV	television
UNDP	United Nations Development Programme
USAID	United States Agency for International Development
WDI	World Development Indicators
WGI	Worldwide Governance Indicators
WTO	World Trade Organization

Index